HISTORIC
COACHING INNS
of the
GREAT
NORTH ROAD

Published by the Campaign for Real Ale Ltd,
230 Hatfield Road, St Albans,
Hertfordshire, AL1 4LW.
www.camra.org.uk/camrabooks

Design and layout © Campaign for Real Ale 2017.
Text © Roger Protz

ISBN 978-1-85249-339-4

A CIP catalogue record for this book is available from the British Library.

Head of Publishing: Simon Hall
Project editors: Katie Button, Julie Hudson
Editorial assistance: Emma Haines
Book design: Hannah Moore.
Maps & illustrations: Hannah Moore.
Typeset in: Cheltenham, Frutiger Capitals, Garamond, Gill Sans,
Zaragoza & Knockout

Printing: Printed and bound in the UK by Cambrian Printers Ltd.,
Aberystwyth.

Disclaimer: Every effort has been made to ensure the contents of this book
are correct at the time of printing. Nevertheless, the Publisher cannot be held
responsible for any errors or omissions, or for changes in any details given, or for
the consequences of any reliance on the information provided by the same. This
does not affect your statutory rights. It is inevitable that some pubs will change
their character during the currency of the book.

HISTORIC COACHING INNS

of the

GREAT NORTH ROAD

*A guide to travelling the
legendary highway*

ROGER PROTZ

BOOKS

Contents

Pictures from left to right: White Horse, Welwyn; The Stagecoach by William Hogarth, 1747; Olde Starre, York; Tolbooth Tavern, Edinburgh; Coach & Horses, Soho; Golden Fleece, York

Introduction

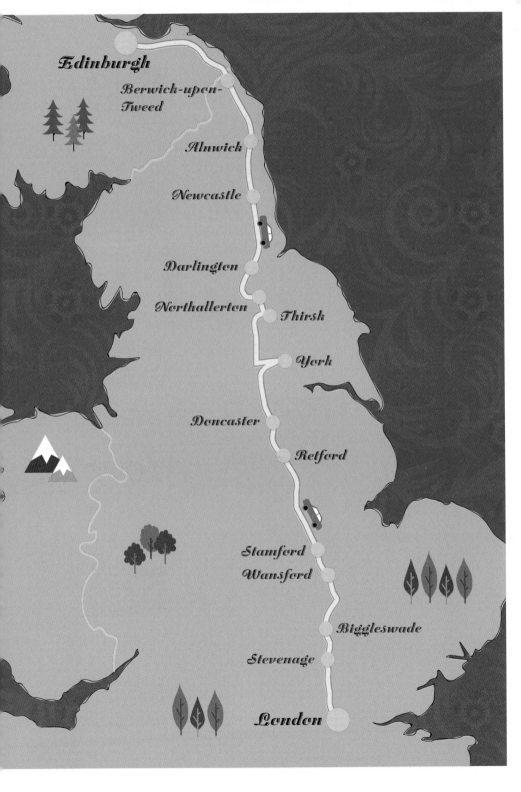

At one place they had to slow down a little, and then Oakroyd read the words painted in large black letters on a whitewashed wall. THE GREAT NORTH ROAD. They were actually going down the Great North Road. He could have shouted. He didn't care what happened after this. He could hear himself telling somebody – Lily it ought to be – all about it. 'Middle o' t'night,' he was saying, 'so we got on to t' Great North Road'. Here was another town, and the road was cutting through it like a knife through cheese. Doncaster, it was. No trams now; everybody gone to bed, except the lucky ones going down South on the Great North Road. – JB Priestley, *The Good Companions*, 1929.

America has Route 66, France L'Autoroute du Soleil and Italy L'Autostrada del Sole. In Britain we have to make do with the more prosaic A1 and its more recent A1(M) motorway sections. But that road grew out of the Great North Road and, as Priestley observed, it was a name that was deeply evocative, creating a feeling of something almost mystical, rooted in our island's history. It can certainly lay claim to be ancient. If the A1 developed out of the Great North Road, that in turn followed an even earlier route dug by the Romans when they were the conquerors of large parts of the British Isles. The Romans built roads for military reasons, to move troops at speed to put down revolts by local tribes, but trade inevitably followed in the wake of the soldiers.

The Great North Road may lack the spectacular scenery that surrounds the famous American, French and Italian roads – though the final stretches through Northumberland and the Borders have some breathtaking backdrops – but it makes up for that with its history. Following in the Romans' footsteps, it has been used by troops preparing to do battle in the Wars of the Roses and the English Civil War and it continued to act as a vital artery for moving military equipment to ward off possible invasions during the 18th, 19th and 20th centuries.

But the road's primary use has been to transport first mail and then people, travelling for work and pleasure – though, as we shall see, pleasure was often in short supply due to the extreme discomfort of coach journeys. The word travel comes from the French *travail*, meaning hard labour, and it was certainly hard pounding on the road north and south. It was also hazardous due to both the weather and the constant threats posed by robbers, highwaymen and ne'er-do-wells.

When the Romans left Britain, their roads were abandoned, left to decay and disappear under soil and rock. The church came to their rescue, improving these ancient pathways to enable monks and pilgrims to visit, go on retreat or pay penance in abbeys and monasteries throughout the land. But the roads remained rudimentary. It was the first Turnpike Act of 1663 that enabled investment to be made in important highways to allow trade to flourish. It authorised the placing of a tollgate at Stilton in Cambridgeshire among other places. The preamble to the Act speaks of the road as 'the ancient highway and post-road leading from London to York and so into Scotland.' The movement of goods between the capitals of England and Scotland was one of the essential elements of the transition from an agrarian economy to a modern one based on trade and manufacture. Later Acts not only allowed for tolls but also for Turnpike Trusts to be set up to collect the tolls and keep the roads in a state of good repair.

The story of the inns on the Great North Road begins with Henry VIII. He was keen to develop a swift and efficient delivery service for the post; it was necessary, after all, for his subjects to learn to whom he was currently joined in matrimony. In 1516 he created the role of Master of the Posts and soon post boys, in bright and distinctive livery, were hammering up and down the road from London, and basic inns sprang up to accommodate them and enable them to change their horses. Stables were built to house horses, which were limited to journeys of a few miles. We will dismiss in the feature on highwaymen (p.112) the absurd notion that Dick Turpin could have ridden from London to York on Black Bess.

In his *Itinerary*, published in 1617, Fynes Morison wrote of the early days of posting: 'In England, towards the south, and in the west parts, and from London to Barwick [Berwick] upon the confines of Scotland, post-horses are established at every ten miles or thereabouts, which they ride a false gallop after some ten miles an hour sometimes, and that makes their hire the greater; for with a commission from the chief postmaster or chiefe lords of the council (given either upon publike businesses, or at least pretence thereof), a passenger shall pay twopence halfpenny each miles for his horse, and as much for his guide's horse; but one mile will serve the whole company, though many ride together, who may easily bring back the horses, driving them before him, who "know the waye as well as a beggar knows his dishe".' [Morison went on to say:] 'This extraordinary charge of

Mail coach starting from the General Post Office in Lombard Street

horses' hire may well be recompenced with the speede of the journey, whereby greater expences in the innes are avoided; all the difficulty is, to have a body able to endure the toyle. For these horses the passenger is at no charge to give them meat onely at the ten miles, and the boy that carries them backe will expect some few pence in gift.' Guides were men mounted on horses who accompanied the post boys to protect them from attack by robbers and to show them the route if they were new to it. Ten miles an hour was impressive, as the average speed of horse-drawn coaches was only seven miles an hour.

James I built on the innovation of Henry VIII by improving the postal service between London and Edinburgh. He was James VI of Scotland before the union of the two countries and was keen to keep a close eye on his subjects north of the border to ward off any possible insurrections against the Sassenachs. The first post office in London was established in 1643 by Charles I and, following the Restoration in 1660, Charles II created the General Post Office, with its headquarters at St Martin's-le-Grand in the City of London. Mail coaches and then passenger coaches left for the north from the GPO and from Hick's Hall at Smithfield, with its large market where drovers brought cattle and sheep from country areas.

A stagecoach service from London to

York and Edinburgh began in 1658. The coach left once a fortnight and it took four days to reach York at a cost of £2. Any hardy traveller who went on for several more days to reach the Scottish capital paid £4. Seen through modern eyes, it was painfully slow. In 1734 the speed of the journey had not improved. John Dale in Edinburgh advertised his coach service as leaving Scotland for London 'towards the end of each week, to be performed in nine days'. Passengers needed comfort to withstand the rigours of such journeys and the small inns for post boys were extended while new and more palatial ones were built to provide much-needed soft beds, hot water, hearty meals and flowing ale.

In the early days of coach and mail transport, few made the journey as far as Edinburgh. One post boy arrived in Scotland with just a single letter in his satchel. York was the preferred destination. As early as 1698 the Black Swan inn in York started a coach service in the spring – there was no service during the winter – as the following announcement, found in a drawer in the inn many years later, made clear:

YORK Four Days Stage-Coach.

Begins on Friday the 12th of April 1706

ALL that are defirous to pafs from *London* to *York*, or from *York* to *London*, or any other Place on that Road; Let them Repair to the *Black Swan* in *Holbourn* in *London*, and to the *Black Swan* in *Coney-ftreet* in *York*.

At both which places they may be received in a Stage Coach every *Monday*, *Wednefday*, and *Friday* which performs the whole Journey in Four Days (*if God permits*). And sets forth at Five in the Morning.

And returns from *York* to *Stamford* in two days, and from *Stamford* by *Huntington* to *London* in two days more. And the like Stages on their return.

Allowing each paffenger 14l. weight, and above 3d. a Pound.

Performed By
{
Benjamin Kingman.
Henry Harrifon.
Walter Bayne's.
}

There are still many fine examples of coaching inns along the Great North Road but, as a result of 'urban renewal', most have long since disappeared in both London and Edinburgh. In London, in the area of St Martin's-le-Grand and Hicks Hall, travellers could be put up at such inviting and luxurious galleried inns as the Bull and Mouth, the Spread Eagle, the Swan with Two Necks and the Green Man and Still. The Bull and Mouth, in a street of the same name, was owned by Edward Sherman who gave up his job as a stockbroker to take over the inn, an indication of the considerable income that could be made from the coaching trade. The enormous underground stables at the Bull and Mouth became one of the great sights of London and from this inn mail and passenger coaches set forth for Edinburgh and Aberdeen via Ferrybridge and Newcastle; Shrewsbury and Holyhead; Birmingham; Leeds; and Leicester.

But Sherman was small beer compared to William Chaplin who built a huge coaching business at the Swan with Two Necks in Gresham Street. Chaplin started his career as a coachman and having earned his spurs went on to become the biggest coach proprietor in England. He accumulated half a million pounds and at the height of the coaching period he owned not only a fleet of carriages but 2,000 horses as well. No less than 27 mail coaches left London every night and Chaplin provided the horses for 14 of them. Coaches left the Swan with Two Necks for Carlisle, Birmingham, Chester, Coventry, Liverpool and Manchester. He didn't panic when the railway arrived in the 1840s but threw in his lot with the new system. He became the deputy chairman of the London and Southampton Railway and increased his influence as the Member of Parliament for Salisbury. He sold off his coaching interests to set up a business with Benjamin Horne who had run a coaching service from the Golden Cross inn at Charing Cross. The new company, Chaplin and Horne, had the exclusive rights to handle goods, including mail and parcels, on the London and Birmingham Railway. It was claimed that Chaplin and Horne were secretly paid £10,000 by the railway company to shut down their coaching concerns, as the railway proprietors were anxious to encourage travellers to use the new mode of transport.

Chaplin at one stage also owned the Spread Eagle inn in Gracechurch Street. Other lost London inns that serviced the Great North Road included the Green Man and Still at the junction of Oxford Street and Argyll Street; the George and Blue Boar in Holborn, where a famous coach, the Stamford Regent, started; and the Saracen's Head in Snow Hill, described as a 'galleried inn of picturesqueness and antiquity' and which dated from the early 16th century. The latter was managed by the

The Spread Eagle in Gracechurch Street, one of London's many lost coaching inns. William Chaplin, who ran a huge coaching business from London, once owned this inn. His name can be seen etched below the eagle.

splendidly named Sarah Ann Mountain who supplied coaches that ran to Carlisle and Penrith via Doncaster, Ferrybridge and Greta Bridge, which means it was the service used by Wackford Squeers when he took his pupils to Dotheboys Hall in Charles Dickens' *Nicholas Nickleby*. Coaches also ran from the Saracen's Head to Hull, Liverpool, Manchester, Birmingham and Shrewsbury. Mrs Mountain was an extremely shrewd businesswoman. She built coaches as well as running them, and hired them out to other carriers, making a handsome income as a result.

In *The Great North Road: London to York*, published in 1901, Charles G Harper said, 'There was no more expressive sight in the London of the beginning of the 19th-century than the simultaneous starting of the mails every evening from the General Post Office. Londoners and country-cousins alike were never weary of the spectacle of the smart coaches, the businesslike

The 16th-century Saracen's Head in Snow Hill, London, sadly now long gone

The mails starting from the General Post Office, 1832

coachmen, and the resplendent, scarlet-coated guards preparing to travel through the night, north, south, east, or west, with His Majesty's mails. Even the passengers shone with the reflected glory, and felt important as, one after the other, the 27 mails began at the stroke of eight o'clock to move off from the double file that filled the street.'

From Hick's Hall it was one mile to the coaches' next destination, the Angel, Islington, its name taken from the great inn there. In fact, there were three inns at the junction reached along Goswell Road, the others being the Peacock and the Queen's Head. All have been lost, though JD Wetherspoon has opened a pub there called the Angel to mark the historic importance of the area: it doesn't, however, continue the 19th-century practice of one Islington pub that refused admittance to 'Gentlemen

with Nails in their Boots'. The Angel had the first tollgate on the way out of London and it was here that both Nicholas Nickleby and Tom Brown joined coaches en route to their respective places of education, where young Tom fared rather better than Nicholas.

The coaches continued from the Angel along what is now called Upper Street and then turned left into the long stretch of the Holloway Road. The road today is densely packed with houses, shops, a department store, pubs, restaurants and a large cinema complex but during the coaching period it was a desolate, open area called the Hollow Way, a low road filled with rubble and water. It was also infested with footpads (robbers) who made every effort to stop coaches and rob the passengers, which is why armed guards accompanied the coaches. Coachmen and passengers must have felt considerable relief when they reached the end of Holloway Road and started the next stage to Highgate, but here they faced a hazard of a different nature: the steep climb up to Highgate Village, 350 feet (107 metres) above sea level. The climb starts at what is now called the Archway, with an Underground station and a large hospital, the Whittington, named after a folk hero, Dick Whittington. Dick, escaping from ill-treatment at his master's house in London in the 14th century, paused with his cat in Highgate and heard Bow Bells tolling the message 'Turn again, Whittington, Thrice Lord Mayor of London'. He accepted the invitation. Centuries later, the coachmen heard no such appeal and so started the long, hard slog up to Highgate. So bad was the road that there were plans to dig a tunnel through to the top of the hill. This was abandoned when the tunnel collapsed and it was accepted that London's thick clay made the enterprise impossible. Instead a new route was built in 1813, Archway Road, which reduced the journey to Highgate by a mile and was 100 feet (30 metres) lower than Highgate Hill. Archway Road was built by a private company and it charged such heavy tolls that many coach companies preferred to stay on the old road. What that stretch of the road was like for passengers can be seen in the opening chapter of Dickens' *A Tale of Two Cities*. He was describing the Old Dover Road to the coast but getting up Shooters Hill in south London must have been identical to attempting to reach Highgate Village:

'He walked up the hill in the mire by the side of the mail, as the rest of the passengers did; not because they had the least relish for walking exercise, under the circumstances, but because the hill, and the harness, and the mud, and the mail, were all so heavy, that the horses had three times already come to a stop, besides once drawing the coach across the road, with mutinous intent of taking it back to Blackheath...With drooping heads and tremulous tails, they mashed their way through the thick mud, floundering and stumbling between whiles, as if they were falling to pieces at the larger joints...Two other passengers, besides the one, were plodding up the hill by the side of the mail. All three were wrapped to the cheekbones and over the ears, and wore jack-boots...

'Once more, the Dover mail struggled on, with the jack-boots of its passengers squishing along by its side. They had stopped when the coach stopped, and they kept close company with it...The last burst carried the mail to the summit of the hill. The horses stopped to breathe again, and the guard got down to skid the wheel for the descent, and open the coach-door to let the passengers in.'

Dickens travelled widely by coach so we can assume this description comes from first-hand experience and isn't fiction. Walking in the bitter cold rather than being carried was indeed hard *travail*. The novelist must have welcomed the arrival of the railway, and its comparative speed and comfort, until he was involved in a serious train accident at Staplehurst in Kent in 1865 in which 10 people were killed and 40 were injured. As a result, did he look back more fondly on the days of the coach?

In Thomas Hughes' *Tom Brown's Schooldays*, Tom, travelling from London to Rugby via the Great North Road, was able to see both the pleasurable and the inhospitable side of coach travel: 'It was another affair altogether, a dark ride on the top of the Tally-Ho, I can tell you, in a light Petersham coat, and your feet dangling six inches from the floor. Then you knew what cold was, and what

it was to be without legs, for not a bit of feeling had you in them after the first half-hour. But it had its pleasures, the old dark ride. First there was the consciousness of silent endurance, so dear to every Englishman – of standing out against something and not giving in. Then there was the music of the rattling harness, and the ring of the horses' feet on the hard road, and the glare of the two bright lamps through the steaming hoar frost, over the leaders' ears, into the darkness; and the cheery toot of the guard's horn, to warn some drowsy pikeman or the hostler at the next change; and the looking forward to daylight, and last, but not least, the delight of returning sensation in your toes.'

How welcome the coaching inns must have been to cold and weary travellers and how they would have agreed with the lines of William

George, Stamford

A re-enactment of the 1840 mail coach arriving at the George in Stamford. The coach shown in this recreation can be seen at the Stockwood Discovery Centre in Luton (see feature on p.56).

Shenstone that were often repeated with affection by that inveterate traveller Dr Samuel Johnson:

Whoe'er has travelled life's dull round,
Where'er his stages may have been,
May sigh to think how oft he found,
The warmest welcome – at an Inn.

And now, reaching Highgate, we can leave behind the sadness of all the lost coaching inns in London and begin to marvel at those that have survived. Sir Walter Scott, who regularly stayed at the George in Stamford, the most famous of all the inns on the Great North Road, said the view of the town's honey-coloured buildings was one of the finest in the country. Our journey takes us to towns and cities with some breathtaking old hostelries with ancient beams, inglenooks, blazing fires, creaking stairs, pewter tankards and a fair share of ghosts. The journey is not an exercise in nostalgia but an attempt to bring greater attention and appreciation to buildings of historic importance. Much of that history is encapsulated in these ancient inns. The remarkable Prince Rupert in Newark, for example, with its half-timbered exterior and vaulted top storey, recalls the ravages of the Civil War in a town where parliamentarians and royalists engaged in long and bloody battles. The Angel & Royal in Grantham is a reminder of an even earlier period with the vast King's Chamber where Richard III signed the warrant for the

Prince Rupert, Newark

Angel & Royal, Grantham

The King's Chamber at the Angel & Royal, Grantham

Tolbooth Tavern, Edinburgh

death of the Earl of Buckingham. The Tolbooth in Edinburgh also featured in the Civil War when the contagion crossed the border while Presbyterian Covenanters were imprisoned there and executed outside. These and many of the other inns along the route are more than just places to eat and drink but are an integral part of Britain's often turbulent history.

It's remarkable and heart-warming that so many have survived, for the arrival of the railway in the 1840s put a swift end to coach travel. Some coaching lingered on for 20 years but most carriers quickly gave up. They simply could not compete with trains that took seven hours to go from London to Edinburgh

rather than nine days. Trains offered comfort and warmth as well as speed and – remarkable though it may seem – were cheaper than coaches. The indefatigable Charles G Harper worked out the comparative costs of train and coach travel. The coaching companies had to pay tolls and taxes, horses, and wages for coachmen, guards, ostlers and helpers. On a long journey, seven coachmen would be needed, with guards to protect them. And passengers, as well as paying fares, also had the price of accommodation to meet. While fares on coach and train were broadly similar, coach travellers had all the additional costs of meals and tips for drivers, ostlers and guards, along with waiters, housemaids and other servants at the inns – and woe betide the traveller who failed to tip his coach driver! Harper estimates that tips added 15 guineas to the cost of a coach trip from London to Edinburgh for a passenger travelling inside and 11 guineas for an 'outsider'.

In spite of the massive cost of building railways, running costs were comparatively low, with fewer employees. Once a passenger had paid for his or her ticket, hotel accommodation, if necessary, would probably only be for one night and the number of meals needed en route were few. Apart from porters, tips were few and far between as passengers rarely had contact with drivers. Coach or train? To use a modern expression, it was a no-brainer and soon the Station Hotel was replacing the George & Dragon.

It is our good fortune that so many of the inns still stand. It has been my pleasure to seek them out and pass them on to you. I have not included every inn along the route. A couple were inexplicably closed during normal pub licensing hours and there were limits to how many times I could drive up and down the A1. A few have been modernised out of all recognition: one inn in South Yorkshire has been knocked through and turned into a 'youth venue', complete with karaoke. Dickens, Johnson and Scott would be rotating in their tombs.

But there are great pleasures ahead.

I have diverted from the A1, created in 1921, with motorway sections added from the 1990s, to visit towns and cities now bypassed by the modern road, York being a prime example. And the old road, eulogised by JB Priestley in 1929, lives on in our memories. An album by Sting in 2016 includes *Heading South on the Great North Road*, a tribute to artists from north-east England who drove to London in search of fame and fortune:

Many have gone before us now,
Many have tried and failed somehow.
Many a soul on the Queen's highway,
Where many a tail light glowed,
With the promise of a better life,
Heading South on the Great North Road,
South on the Great North Road.

Enjoy the journey!

Roger Protz
St Albans
February 2017

1

London to Stevenage

Mulberry Tree, Stevenage

A1

Biggleswade

Stevenage
11 Mulberry Tree

White Horse, Welwyn

A1 (M)

Welwyn
10 White Horse
9 Wellington
8 White Hart

Hatfield
7 Eight Bells

North Finchley & Barnet
6 Duke of York
5 Olde Mitre

A1000

A1

London

Highgate & Hampstead
4 Spaniards Inn
3 Duke's Head
2 Bull & Last

Soho
1 Coach & Horses

Coach & Horses, Soho

*P*ost boys, royalty, aristocracy, great writers and young men seeking higher education all joined forces to board coaches at St Martin's-le-Grand, Smithfield and the Angel, Islington, to head north. It was slow progress at first, with steep, rutted roads leading to Highgate and an equally challenging clamber to Barnet. The terrain became easier once the coaches passed Hatfield. It was no less hazardous, however, as this first stretch of the Great North Road was fertile ground for highwaymen seeking to line their pockets at travellers' expense.

Soho, London
(423 miles to Edinburgh)

We begin our journey in the heart of London's West End, famous for Theatreland, Chinatown, Piccadilly Circus, Ronnie Scott's jazz club and, above all, for Soho, where we take our first pause for refreshment. It's an area with a fascinating past and present. The name Soho is thought to come from the time when the area was open fields and hunting took place there; horsemen and hounds were called to order by the shout of 'Soho'. It has been a melting pot of immigrants, including French Huguenots fleeing persecution in the late 17th century, followed by the arrival of large numbers of Greeks and Italians in the 1800s, which led to a proliferation of restaurants and cafes in the area. In the post-World War Two era, Soho became notorious for sleazy sex cinemas and prostitution but it's since been gentrified and is now a centre for the film industry and good restaurants. Soho's also long been a haunt of artists, writers and journalists, some of whom – Dylan Thomas, George Melly and the infamous Jeffrey Bernard – have left their boozy mark on the area. Jeffrey Bernard's favourite watering hole in Soho was the Coach & Horses and it is here that our journey commences.

❶ Coach & Horses
29 Greek Street, London, W1D 5DH
020 7437 5920

The Coach & Horses played an important role in the coach trade in the 18th and 19th century. The pub is Grade

II listed, was originally built in the 18th century and rebuilt in 1856 with a striking wedge-shaped, red-pillared exterior. The pub's name stems from the fact that it offered a special service to customers who had to catch a stagecoach along the Great North Road. It was a similar service to the one offered today by hotels close to airports that pick up passengers by bus. The Coach & Horses would take customers by small horse-drawn carriages from Soho to the starting point for the north at Smithfield, a short and relatively swift journey from the West End to the Clerkenwell area. There is also the possibility that coaches may have begun the main journey to York from the Soho inn. The entry for

Boroughbridge in Yorkshire (on p.134) includes an advertisement for coaches plying the London to Edinburgh route starting from the Coach & Horses in Dean Street, Soho: there were, however, several inns in the area at the time that were known by that name.

The pub has a chequered history as a result of its habitués in recent years. Emblazoned on the pub sign is the single word 'Norman's', topped by an artillery gun. The gun is the logo of Taylor Walker, a long dead London brewery but whose name is still used by the present owners, and the weapon is a suitable symbol for the notorious, now retired, landlord Norman Balon. He was known as – and was proud of his infamy – the rudest pub landlord in London. He underscored the fact by calling his memoirs *You're Barred, You Bastards*. Among those he regularly evicted was the notorious womaniser, gambler and old soak Jeffrey Bernard. From 1976, Bernard wrote a weekly column, 'Low Life', for the *Spectator* magazine and from time to time his column was missing with an apologetic editorial note: 'Jeffrey Bernard is unwell', a euphemism for his state of total inebriation. Eventually the writer Keith Waterhouse turned Bernard's writing and follies into a long-running and acclaimed West End play *Jeffrey Bernard Is Unwell*, starring Peter O'Toole. It was reprised when Bernard died in 1997. Among the many pictures, cartoons and photos in the pub is one of O'Toole as

Bernard. There's also a famous photo of the late Queen Mother pulling a pint of beer, but this didn't take place in the Coach & Horses as the beer in question is Young's. What does regularly feature here is the fortnightly lunch organised by the satirical magazine *Private Eye*, which is based in Soho: the wood-panelled walls are liberally dotted with cartoons from the magazine.

The pub sells several Fuller's beers and I enjoyed a glass of Hopspur from the Redemption brewery in Tottenham. Behind the bar you will spot ancient logos for Double Diamond and Skol, keg beer and lager from the 1970s that are mercifully no longer with us. The pub now specialises in vegetarian and vegan food. I can imagine what Jeffrey Bernard would have said about that, but it wouldn't be printable.

Clerkenwell, London
(422 miles to Edinburgh)

The carriages from Soho deposited their customers at Smithfield, where we can now begin our journey proper. Smithfield Market was the original starting point for the Great North Road and coaches left there to pick up further passengers at the Angel, Islington. This major road junction takes its name from one of the most famous old inns in London. It started life as a modest tavern in the 16th century on land called the Sheepcote that belonged to Clerkenwell Priory. It became a fully-fledged inn by the end of the 16th century and was named the Angel after the Angel of the Annunciation, whose image appeared on the inn sign. The opening of the New Road in 1756 brought more traffic to the area and, while the Angel was the biggest inn in the area, several others competed for trade. Customers included not only coach passengers but also

The Stagecoach by William Hogarth, 1747, believed to be based in the grounds of the Angel, Islington

livestock traders driving their herds to Smithfield Market.

Fictional characters who stayed at the Angel included Tom Brown and Nicholas Nickleby as they prepared to head north to improve their education. It's claimed Thomas Paine started to write *The Rights of Man*, which defended the French Revolution, at the Angel in 1790, though a similar claim is made by the Old Red Lion a few yards away in St John Street. The Old Red Lion is now a celebrated theatre pub but the Angel ceased to be a coaching inn as trade dwindled and it was sold in 1896 to the East London brewer Truman. In the 20th century it became a restaurant and then offices, and now houses a branch of the Co-op Bank. It was saved from demolition and is now a Grade II-listed building, part of the Angel Conservation Area. Its history as an inn is marked by a modern Wetherspoon pub called the Angel and it gives its name to an underground station on the Northern Line.

Highgate and Hampstead, London
(417 miles to Edinburgh)

To find some existing coaching inns in London we have to head for Highgate. The road rises steeply and when it was rutted and muddy it took its toll on both coaches and passengers, making frequent stops necessary to change the horses.

 ## Bull & Last

168 Highgate Road, London, NW5 1QS
020 7267 3641 www.thebullandlast.co.uk

The Bull & Last dates from the early 18th century and it was rebuilt in the 1840s following a fire. It was first called simply the Bull and adopted the current titles as a result of coachmen telling passengers, who had survived the journey from the north, that the inn was the last one before London, at a time when Highgate was a small rural village. Two bulls' heads hang rather alarmingly behind the bar, further evidence perhaps that drovers would have stopped there en route to Smithfield. A different school of thought argues that 'bull' is much older, derived from *bulla*, the Latin term for the lead seal attached to Papal edicts. Whatever its origins, the Bull & Last is an imposing three-storey, street-corner building rich in plant life outside.

It was taken over in 2008 by a trio of Freddie Fleming, Ollie Pudney and Joe Swiets who turned it into one of the most fashionable eating places in North London. I'm not a fan of 'gastropubs', as all too often they cease to be pubs and

Bull & Last, Highgate

turn into restaurants. But, as I pushed through the heavy drapes at the entrance, my first sight was a man sitting at the bar, nursing a pint and reading a newspaper. That makes it a pub in my book, and there's a good choice of handpumped beers on the bar, including, on my visit, ales from Arbor, Burning Sky, Park and Wild Weather breweries. The Bull & Last's ground floor has scrubbed wood floors, a wood-slatted ceiling, tables set aside for either eating or drinking, and an open fire at the far end, topped by a large mirror. The room is dominated by a vast map on the wall, showing the area during the heyday of coach travel. Another large room on the first floor is devoted to serious dining but customers are encouraged to eat in the bar. The extensive menu includes Jerusalem artichoke soup, wild game terrine, Lyonnaise salad with eel, roast beef salad, wild mushroom rigatoni, and chargrilled steaks.

Duke's Head, Highgate

❸ Duke's Head

16 Highgate High Street, London, N6 5JG
020 8341 1310 www.thedukesheadhighgate.co.uk

By coaching inn standards, the Duke's Head in Highgate village is a small tavern, the wide entrance for coaches dominating the facade. Inside it's been modernised in a sensitive and tasteful fashion, grey-green walls melding with the flagstone floors. It has very low ceilings and wooden settles, and a long bar running almost the length of the building with a vast selection of both handpumped real ales and craft keg beers, all listed on boards.

It's a shrine to good beer and not surprisingly it's regularly listed in the *Good Beer Guide* and has won awards from the local branch of CAMRA. The beer choice changes almost daily but ales from Hammerton are a fixture

Highgate and Horns

Highgate pubs are infamous for the bizarre ceremony known as the Swearing on the Horns, which dates from at least the 17th century and continues today in the Flask, the Wrestlers and other local pubs. Pubs had antlers tied to a pole placed outside to indicate when the ceremony was taking place and visitors were invited to chant promises that they would eat white bread in preference to brown, drink strong ale rather than 'small' [weak] beer, and not kiss the maid if the mistress were present 'but sooner than miss a chance, kiss them both'. Lord Byron referred to the ceremony in *Childe Harold's Pilgrimage*:

Many to the steep of Highgate hie;
Ask, ye Boeotian shades! The reason why?
'Tis to the worship of the solemn Horn,
Grasped in the holy land of Mystery.
In whose dread name both men and maids are sworn.
And consecrate the oath with draught and dance till morn.

and you may also find the likes of Beavertown, Brixton, Burning Sky, Five Points, Kernel, Magic Rock, Moor and Waen. The inn specialises in 'pop-up' and street food, supplied by outside suppliers. On my visit the street food had a strong Caribbean influence and the menu included fried chicken wings, rum jerk halloumi, curried goat, creole aubergine, coconut and thyme corn on the cob, coconut stew, fried plantain, and pearl barley pilaf. This is not traditional coaching inn 'scoff', to use a London expression, but it was delicious and an ideal companion for hoppy and quenching ales.

④ Spaniards Inn

Spaniards Road, Hampstead, London, NW3 7JJ
020 8731 8406 www.thespaniardshampstead.co.uk

The Spaniards Inn is just off the Great North Road but is worth a small diversion to enjoy its atmosphere, rich history, literary connections and proximity to both Kenwood House and Hampstead Heath. Spaniards Road is a continuation of Hampstead Lane and the inn has its own bus stop: catch the 210 from Highgate Village, though it's a pleasant stroll along the undulating road, with impressive villas on either side.

The Spaniards is so steeped in history that I felt, as I made my notes, I should use a quill pen and wear a periwig. Charles Dickens drank there and mentioned it in *The Pickwick Papers*. Bram Stoker apparently took inspiration from the inn's ghostly past when writing Dracula. It's claimed, without firm foundation, that John Keats wrote *An Ode to a Nightingale* in the inn's garden when he heard the bird singing there. Fittingly, there are benches at the front of the inn with Dickens' and Keats' names engraved on them.

Inside you will find a ramble of wood-panelled rooms, low ceilings held up by standing posts, blazing fires in winter, and a tiny snug as you enter with space for just two or three people. The floors are of polished wood and settles of both wood and leather provide comfortable seating. Creaking stairs lead up to the first floor dining and function

The cosy snug at the Spaniards with room for three

room, which has a portrait of Keats.

The inn was built in 1585 as a tollgate, marking the entrance to the Bishop of London's estate. An original boundary stone from 1755 is in the pub garden and the Spaniards still marks the boundary between the boroughs of Barnet and Camden: the inn is in Barnet while the toll house on the other side of the road is in Camden. Both buildings are Grade II listed and a move to demolish the toll house to widen the road in the 1960s was resisted.

The origins of the name are disputed. Some say it was the home of the Spanish Ambassador to the court of James I. A different tale says it was run by two Spaniards, Francesco and Juan Perero in

the 18th century, who fought a duel over a woman. Juan was killed and he now haunts the inn, along with a woman in white seen in the garden, a moneylender knocked down by a coach on the road, and highwayman Dick Turpin. It's claimed, without foundation, that his father was once the landlord and Turpin used the inn as a hiding place from his pursuers and stabled Black Bess in the toll house.

The Spaniards has seen its fair amount of turmoil and upheaval. During the anti-Catholic Gordon Riots in London in 1780, the landlord of the inn, Giles Thomas, saved Kenwood House and its collection of paintings from being torched by the mob. He gave them such copious amounts of ale that they were rendered too drunk to continue their mayhem and Thomas was able to call up the cavalry to arrest them. Today the inn is a haven of peace and quiet. In warm weather, the garden is a delight, lit by multi-coloured small lamps in the evening. You can eat well with such dishes as sautéed mushrooms, baby kale salad, scallops, fish and chips, mushroom risotto, burgers and steaks, and a cheese board that includes Mrs Kirkham's Lancashire. The beers have changed a tad since Dickens and Keats quaffed on the benches at the front. Today you will find Dark Star Hop Head, Fuller's London Pride, Hogs Back TEA and Sharp's Doom Bar.

Famous Guests There is a long list of artistic and literary luminaries who visited the Spaniards including the painters Constable, Turner and Reynolds, and writers and poets Lord Byron, Dickens, Keats, William Blake, Robert Louis Stevenson and Mary Shelley.

On the area

Highgate Cemetery (Swain's Lane, N6 6PJ; 020 8340 1834; www.highgatecemetery.org) – best known as the resting place of Karl Marx, but you will also find the graves of Christina Rossetti, Michael Faraday, George Eliot and Charles Dickens' parents.

Kenwood House (Hampstead Lane, NW3 7JR; 020 8348 1286; www.english-heritage.org.uk/kenwood) – a former stately home owned for many years by the ennobled branch of the Guinness family, the Iveaghs, and now managed by English Heritage. Robert Adam designed the house and gardens and the collection of artwork includes paintings by Gainsborough, Landseer, Rembrandt, Reynolds, Turner and Van Dyck.

Hampstead Heath – North London's sylvan playground with inspirational views over the capital.

North Finchley and Barnet

(412 miles to Edinburgh)

From Highgate Village our journey continues along the Great North Road to the next important stop in Barnet. But en route it's important to pause at Tally Ho Corner in North Finchley as it plays an important role as both a coach stop and the haunt of highwaymen. The corner is the junction of Ballards Lane and the Great North Road and takes its name from the Tally Ho coach company, formed in 1830, which stabled 16 horses there. The junction has an impressive, three-storey, gabled pub called the Tally Ho, which was built in 1927 and is therefore outside our brief.

Tally Ho Corner was built on part of Finchley Common, which in the 18th century was a dangerous area, with highwaymen stationed there to 'touch the mails' as the coaches went by. The Whig politician and writer Edmund Burke was apprehended on the common in 1774 by two highwaymen who robbed him of 10 guineas and took his servant's watch. Dick Turpin and another notorious highwayman, Jack Sheppard, were active in and around the common and it remained dangerous long after they had been arrested and despatched. In 1790, the Earl of Minto, travelling to London, wrote to his wife that instead of pushing on to town at night he would defer his entry until morning 'for I shall not trust my throat on Finchley Common in the dark.'

Watching out for footpads, we now make the long haul up to High Barnet. High indeed, for the road is steep and must have put a great strain on coaches and horses. Barnet became a major stop for coaches in both directions and at one time it was known as the 'Town of Inns' as a result of the large number of taverns vying for the profits of the trade, with as many as 150 coaches stopping every day. A stroll along the high street shows that many buildings that are now offices and shops were once coaching inns due to the trademark wide, arched entrances alongside. Sadly, very few of the original inns remain. As you enter the main street in Barnet, the Red Lion makes its presence felt, with an animal of that breed jutting out from the top storey of the building. This was one of the principal coaching inns in the town but the present building dates from the 20th century and is not the original, though there are photos and prints of old Barnet on the walls.

⑤ Olde Mitre

58 High Street, Barnet, EN5 5SJ 020 8449 5701

Ye Olde Mitre is a gem that, fortunately, has escaped the ravages of pub company architects and marketing

departments. It's the oldest inn in Barnet and was first licensed in 1553 when it was known as La Roose & La Crown, later La Bush, then the Rose & Crown before taking on its current name, probably due to its proximity to the local church. Since the decline of the coach trade, it has lost its stables and other outbuildings: in its heyday, it had 12 beds for travellers and stabling for 26 horses. The timber-framed main building has been awarded Grade II-listed status and has a superb interior of wood-panelled walls, open fires, low ceilings and a large wooden bar. There are many prints of old Barnet, breweriana and certificates of its awards from CAMRA decorating the walls. In the back room, there's a portrait of Charles Dickens who not only visited the Olde Mitre but also used it as the inn where the Artful

Dodger took Oliver Twist. In 1660, it's claimed that General Monck stayed there en route to London to install Charles II on the throne at the end of Cromwell's Commonwealth. In 1720, the Archdeacon of St Albans entertained 178 justices there – must have been a bit of a squeeze – who met to quell a riot at Barnet Fair. Justice was hard in the 18th century: one ancient print reports that on 5 December 1739 Joseph Eades of Finchley was indicted for the crime of stealing a horsewhip.

Another celebrated visitor was the lexicographer Dr Samuel Johnson in 1774, accompanied by Hester Thrale, the wife of the owner of Thrale's brewery in Southwark: the Thrales were originally from Sandridge near St Albans. Johnson had rooms at the brewery which, as Barclay Perkins, went on to become the

The Duke of York between Barnet and Potters Bar commemorates the Battle of Barnet in 1471

biggest producer of beer in London. Along with good pub food, the Olde Mitre, regularly listed in the *Good Beer Guide*, has an excellent beer range, including Adnams, Deuchars IPA, the sublime Taylor's Landlord and ales from several smaller breweries.

⑥ Duke of York

Ganwick Corner, Barnet Road, Barnet, EN5 4SG
020 8440 4674
www.brunningandprice.co.uk/dukeofyork

This attractive brown-brick building with imposing chimneys has an identity problem. It's officially in Enfield with a London phone number but it's correctly in Hertfordshire and is thought to have once been part of the 2,500 acre Wrotham Hall estate. Wrotham Hall – pronounced 'Rootham' – is the ancestral home of the Earls of Strafford with Palladian buildings dating from 1754 and is firmly and proudly based in Hertfordshire. The movie *Gosford Park* was filmed there.

The inn is owned by the highly regarded specialist pub group Brunning & Price and it has used all its skills to renovate the buildings. It's a mixture of ancient and modern, with wooden floors and heavy oak bars along with a conservatory for dining and a large garden where customers can eat, drink and allow children to use the play facilities. There are old street lamps in the front garden and across the road you can spot an old sign proclaiming the Great North Road. The history of the inn

and the area, including the Battle of Barnet, is displayed on the wood-panelled walls. My only quibble is that the Duke of York attired in a periwig on the pub sign is not the one who led his troops in the battle close by. The duke shown here is the Grand Old one who famously led his troops up the hill and down again.

The food is excellent and includes snacks and sandwiches and a range of

Barnet History

The town is famous for its fair: the name Barnet Fair became part of Cockney rhyming slang and means 'hair', as in 'Nice Barnet, pity about the boat race [face]'. The fair, where horse racing took place and cattle were sold, dated from Tudor times.

The Battle of Barnet took place just north of the town at Monken Hadley on Easter Day in 1471. It marked the beginning of the end of the Wars of the Roses, when the Duke of York, later Edward IV, defeated the Lancastrians led by the Earl of Warwick. An obelisk called Hadley Highstone marks the site of the Barnet battle.

The large garden at the Duke of York, Barnet

dishes on the full menu that includes venison and rabbit, pork belly with quinoa, prawn and squid linguine, and wild mushroom risotto. Beers include Brunning & Price Original, a special ale brewed for the group by the Phoenix Brewery in Lancashire, and a changing range of guest beers that could include Mighty Oak from Essex and Portobello from London.

Hatfield, Hertfordshire
(21 miles from London, 402 miles to Edinburgh)

The Great North Road finally breaks free from the embrace of London and heads into the Home Counties. From Potters Bar, named after a Roman pottery and a bar or tollgate, the road heads past the towering aerials of the BBC's transmitter station at Brookmans Park and a large pub called the Cock of the North, which would be a splendid name for a coaching inn but is, in fact, a more prosaic 20th-century road house. The next stop is Hatfield, a sprawling mix of old and new, once the home of British Aerospace, now occupied by the University of Hertfordshire, and, in the old town, the magnificent Jacobean estate of Hatfield House. The house is the ancestral home of the Cecil family, one of the most powerful political dynasties in English and British history. Robert Cecil, the first Lord Salisbury, who was James I's chief minister, built the house in 1611. It replaced the Royal Palace of Hatfield that was the childhood home of Princess Elizabeth. She visited the house frequently when she became queen but was less than impressed by the ale Lord Salisbury offered there. On one occasion she sent servants back to London to bring ale that was more to her liking. The power of the nobility continued into the 19th century when the Cecils had the Great North Road diverted so it did not disturb their tranquillity. And when the iron horse replaced the stagecoach, they insisted that Hatfield Station should be built across the road from their main gates in order that the third Lord Salisbury, prime minister from 1895 to 1902, would have easy access to London in his own private carriage.

Hatfield's surviving coaching inn is tucked away behind the estate in an area dominated by St Etheldreda's Church and some fine old half-timbered buildings.

❼ Eight Bells

2 Park Street, Hatfield, Hertfordshire, AL9 5AX
01707 272477

The Eight Bells, on the corner of Park Street and Fore Street, is Hatfield's oldest inn. It dates from 1630 and is Grade II listed. It was first called the Five Bells in deference to the church but when the

number was increased to eight the pub's name followed suit. In fact, St Etheldreda's now has ten bells but the pub is content with its eight.

The inn is a delight. As well as a warm welcome from the landlord and landlady, you can marvel at the low beams and standing timbers, wood and slate floors, old settles and two fireplaces. In the 19th century it had three bedrooms for travellers and stabling for four horses: in 1839 a coach called the Sovereign left the inn every day at 7am for London.

It has a rich history. In 1756 the landlord, Will Harrow, supplemented his income from the Eight Bells by doubling as a highwayman, an activity that led to his execution in Hertford in 1763. It's claimed that Dick Turpin also lodged at

In the area

Hatfield House (AL9 5NQ; 01707 287010; www.hatfield-house. co.uk) – stately home open to the public April–September, exhibits include artefacts of the Cecil family and Elizabeth I.

The Comet pub (St Albans Road, Hatfield, AL10 9RH; 01707 265411) – the last link to British Aerospace, which seen from above is shaped like a Comet plane.

Eight Bells, Hatfield

the inn and on one occasion jumped from the top storey on to Black Bess to escape the Bow Street Runners, London's first police force. The number of times Turpin escaped his pursuers in this fashion suggests the poor old nag must have had a deeply bowed back.

Charles Dickens went to the Eight Bells in 1835 when, as a young reporter, he covered the death of the Marchioness of Salisbury who died in a fire at Hatfield House. The inn was the inspiration for the pub in *Oliver Twist* where Bill Sikes sought refuge with his dog after he had killed his lover, Nancy. 'It was nine o'clock at night when the

man, quite tired out, and the dog, limping and lame from the unaccustomed exercise, turned down the hill by the church of the quiet village, and plodded along the little street, crept into a small public-house, whose scanty light had guided them to the spot. There was a fire in the tap-room, and some country labourers were drinking before it.'

The Eight Bells today offers good pub food and a changing range of beers that includes Hobgoblin and St Austell Tribute while a chalk board promised such tempting guest beers as Adnams Ghost Ship and Wells' Bombardier.

Welwyn, Hertfordshire

(27 miles from London, 396 miles to Edinburgh)

It's a short journey along the A1 from Hatfield to Welwyn. Locals call it either Old Welwyn or Welwyn Village to avoid confusion with neighbouring Welwyn Garden City, a 20th century new town devoid of coaching inns. Old Welwyn, on the other hand, despite being tiny, has three and the village was once an important coaching stop on the Great North Road. It's an ancient place that once had Roman baths: it was close to the great Roman settlement of Verulamium, now St Albans. The importance of Welwyn in the 18th and 19th centuries can be measured by the fact that 80 teams of horses a day were handled at one of the coaching inns, the White Hart.

modernised but tastefully so and its walls are decorated with many fascinating images and artefacts of Old Welwyn. The imposing restaurant area, however, has been left in all its old glory, with ancient beams and a vast inglenook fireplace. The food offering is impressive with snacks or full meals that include cheese croquettes, whitebait, trout pâté and soup as starters, and such mains as smoked salmon fish cakes, cod and chips, beer battered halloumi, paprika and lemon chicken, Caesar salad, sea bass, burgers, steaks, and charred cauliflower cheese. The inn is owned by Charles Wells, the Bedford-based family brewery, and the bar offers a selection of its beers.

❽ White Hart

2 Prospect Place, Welwyn, Hertfordshire, AL6 9EN
01438 715353   www.whitehartwelwyn.co.uk

Standing alongside the River Mimram, the White Hart inn dates from 1675. You could sleep where the horses were once fed and watered as some of its 13 bedrooms are in the converted stable block. Several rooms have four-poster beds.

The main entrance to the pub is more recent and the original entrance is now part of the cellar bar and restaurant. The ground floor bar has also been

The courtyard at the White Hart, where coaches would once have halted

⑨ Wellington

1 High Street, Welwyn, Hertfordshire, AL6 9LZ
01438 714036 www.wellingtonatwelwyn.co.uk

The Wellington is in pole position in the village. It's a large and imposing building opposite the church, with an impressive dormer and large entrance that was once the egress for coaches. It has something of an identity crisis: the hanging boot inn sign and a large portrait of the 'Iron Duke' in the rear garden emphasise its links to the Duke of Wellington, who vanquished Napoleon Bonaparte at the Battle of Waterloo in 1815. But that's a more recent name as it was first called the White Swan. It's an inn of great antiquity, dating from the 13th century and, with due respect to the Duke, should have retained its original name. But let's not be mealy-mouthed: the Wellington was badly damaged by fire in 2012 and the owners, Greene King, have restored it with great care and precision and avoided any urge to modernise it.

It's a pleasure to sit inside and marvel at the old beams, wooden floors and open fires. The walls are part bare brick and part slatted wood. There are six bedrooms, reached up creaking wooden stairs: a writer from the *Daily Telegraph* who stayed there praised the facilities in the spacious rooms. The food on offer is wide-ranging and draws a large custom, but booking is not necessary as the management claim is, 'we'll fit you in'. As well as daily specials, there are snacks, sharing platters, fish chowder, ham and eggs, chicken tagliatelle, goat's cheese and beetroot lasagne, and burgers. The beer choice is limited: just Old Speckled Hen and a house beer called Wellington Pale Ale.

As I sat making my notes, I was aware that greater literary figures than me had been regular visitors. Samuel Pepys stayed here, as he regularly journeyed south to London, while Dr Samuel

Johnson was also a frequent visitor during his peregrinations around the country. The famous actor David Garrick also dropped by.

Wellington, Welwyn

⑩ White Horse

30 Mill Lane, Welwyn, Hertfordshire, AL6 9ET
01438 714366 www.thewhitehorse-welwyn.co.uk

Welwyn hasn't finished offering up its delights. A third old coaching inn, the White Horse, dates from 1742 and is now a Grade II-listed building. It has an attractive white facade decked out with hanging baskets and window boxes. Since a recent refurbishment it now promotes itself as a gastro pub but has retained its old beams and exposed brick walls. It prides itself on using local ingredients, including vegetables, for its extensive menu that includes soup, broccoli and goat's cheese salad, baked Camembert, ale-braised ox cheeks, chicken supreme, lobster mac, ravioli with toasted seeds, and vegetable strudel. Beers include Adnams Southwold Bitter, Sharp's Doom Bar and Taylor's Landlord.

The garden at the White Horse, Welwyn with the old stables in the background

The White Horse, Welwyn

Stevenage, Hertfordshire
(33 miles from London, 390 miles to Edinburgh)

Stevenage, in common with Hatfield, Hemel Hempstead and Watford, is a Hertfordshire town with an identity crisis, an odd blend of garish new town and old. Go past the high-rise blocks and a train station with all the charm of a mausoleum and you come to the old town with some history as well as pleasant shops, cafes and restaurants. It has a coaching inn of considerable antiquity and a degree of controversy.

11 Mulberry Tree

60 High Street, Stevenage, Hertfordshire, SG1 3EA
01438 355515 www.themulberrytree-stevenage.co.uk

Founded around 1653, it was called the White Lion but following a major overhaul by Greene King it emerged with a new name: the Mulberry Tree. This outraged local historian Hugh Madgin who said no such tree had ever grown there and added that as the fruit of the tree is hallucinogenic it was an unfortunate

Mulberry Tree, Stevenage

name for Greene King to choose. In the brewer's defence, the 1967 film *Here We Go Round the Mulberry Bush*, about teenage sexual awakenings, was filmed in Stevenage.

Greene King can also be praised for a sensitive refurbishment, leaving intact the ancient beams and timbers of the large and rambling interior. The spacious beer garden to the rear, which was once the entrance for coaches and stabling for horses, is fronted by two white lions, so the original name lives on. The inn played a central role in the local community, acting as fire station and vestry, and hosting local clubs. It also had cellars where French soldiers from the Napoleonic wars were held prisoner before being taken further north by coach to long-term jail.

The White Lion was also a haunt of highwaymen, who met there to plan their robberies. Inevitably, the gang included Dick Turpin but – for this relief, much thanks – it's not claimed he jumped from a top window on to the hapless Black Bess. Instead he and his fellow miscreants escaped using tunnels beneath the inn.

Today, the pub's wide-ranging menu includes sharing platters, nibbles, baked Camembert, macaroni cheese, fish and chips, burgers, shepherd's pie, salads and sausage and mash. Beers are from the Greene King range.

In the area

Knebworth House (SG3 6PY; 01438 812661) – just off the A1, a Tudor mansion that's the ancestral home of the Lytton family. House and gardens are open to the public in the summer and it's also a venue for regular rock concerts: gigs there have featured the Rolling Stones, Paul McCartney, Led Zeppelin, Robbie Williams and Iron Maiden.

Coach collection

What was it like to travel by coach? You can get a graphic view by visiting the remarkable variety of old vehicles that form the Mossman Collection at the Stockwood Discovery Centre in Luton, Bedfordshire. Here you can see all forms of coaches from Tudor times until the 20th century, including many examples of coaches that took mail and passengers along the Great North Road.

The collection was the lifetime achievement of George Mossman from Caddington who built and restored horse-drawn vehicles for more than 50 years. He was born in 1908 and his first job when he left school was with a St Albans butcher for whom he delivered meat using horse-drawn delivery vehicles.

Mossman became a farmer and a businessman but in his spare time built his collection of vehicles and employed skilled craftsmen to restore them on his farm.

He supplied coaches for such important events as the Lord Mayor's Show in London and the coronation of Elizabeth II. As his fame spread, he was called on to supply coaches for many historical films made in Britain and the United States. The collection bequeathed by his family to Luton Museums includes a replica of one the earliest passenger coaches built during the reign of Elizabeth I. Such springless

vehicles would have been horrendously uncomfortable, drawn by teams of horses and oxen over muddy and poorly maintained roads. Until glass was used, coaches were wide open, which meant that even passengers in the 'posh' seats inside were assailed by wind and rain. It was not until roads were improved by the likes of McAdam in the 18th century and coaches were enclosed and properly sprung that travel became relatively comfortable.

One coach in the collection dates from about 1790 and is a fine example of an early stagecoach. It's a four wheeled wagon covered in canvas and it could carry up to 30 passengers. Arguably the finest vehicle on view is the Royal Mail coach circa 1840, with the royal coat of arms on the door: it carried mail and passengers between London and York. These coaches were known as 'mails' and worked night and day along the Great North Road.

Mossman's research shows that the

Royal Mail coach circa 1840

speed of coaches gradually improved from five miles an hour in 1720 to almost 11 miles an hour in the early 19th century. Most coaches travelled 50 or 60 miles a day, with frequent stops at inns to change horses. In 1768 the charge for coach travel was one shilling or five pence.

The most striking vehicle in the collection never travelled along the Great North Road. It's a garishly painted Wells Fargo stagecoach from the American Wild West, where drivers and passengers faced attack not by Dick Turpin and his kind with firearms but by bows and arrows.

Some of the films supplied by Mossman's coaches include the original *Wicked Lady* (1945) starring Margaret Lockwood and a 1983 revival with Faye Dunaway; *Chitty Chitty Bang Bang*; *Around the World in 80 Days*; and one of the last of the Carry On films, *Carry on Dick*, with Sid James playing Dick Turpin.

Stockwood Discovery Centre
(London Road, Luton, LU1 4LX; 01582 548600; www.lutonculture.com/stockwood-discovery-centre) – Entry to the centre and the Mossman Collection is free. As well as the vehicles, there are exhibitions on local history, gardens, a café and a children's play area.

2

Biggleswade to Wansford

Haycock Hotel, Wansford

Stamford

Wansford
20 Haycock Hotel

Bell, Stilton

A1 (M)

Stilton **19** Bell

Alconbury **18** Manor

Brampton **15** Black Bull   *Huntingdon*

Buckden **14** Lion   **17** Falcon

16 George

Eaton Socon

13 White Horse

Biggleswade

12 New Inn

White Horse, Eaton Socon

Stevenage

A1 (M)

he Great North Road rises quite steeply between Hatfield and Stevenage but it's easier terrain once we enter the flatlands of Bedfordshire and Cambridgeshire. It was ideal territory for highwaymen who could hide among the trees that lined the route, making it one of the most dangerous stretches of the road. Charles Dickens immortalised Eaton Socon in Nicholas Nickleby and Henry VIII left his mark on Buckden. Samuel Pepys was a frequent visitor to several inns on this section of the road while the Bell at Stilton can boast not only many celebrity guests but its links to the world's greatest cheese.

Biggleswade, Bedfordshire

(46 miles from London, 377 miles to Edinburgh)

If they arrived unscathed, both coachmen and their passengers would have been relieved to enter Biggleswade with its choice of inns and resting places. There's an old A1 joke that says the town is named after a truck driver called Big Les Wade but Biggleswade has a long history that predates the road. It was linked to the great Roman city of Verulamium, now St Albans, and has been a place of vigorous trade and commerce for centuries, with lords of the manor residing in some splendour in their impressive houses.

But many of the town's historic buildings were lost in the terrible conflagration known as the Great Fire of Biggleswade in 1785. Among the buildings swept away were many of its inns. They were replaced by modern pubs in the 19th and 20th centuries and at one stage Biggleswade had no fewer than 75 of them. The story of the plethora of hostelries is told in a fascinating book, *Thirsty Old Town*, by local historian Ken Page, first published in 1995.

The ancient market square still has some inns that survived the blaze in the 18th century. The White Hart, with an impressive half-timbered exterior, dates from 1678 and is the second oldest inn in the town. The Crown Hotel was built in 1672 and the large arched entrance indicates it was a substantial coaching inn. At the time of writing it was closed.

After a long tussle, Wetherspoon won permission from the local council to reopen the inn and it will no doubt be up to its usual well-run if ubiquitous style.

⑫ New Inn

16a Market Square, Biggleswade, Bedfordshire, SG18 8AS 01767 222938
www.thenewinnalehouseandkitchen.co.uk

In spite of the name, the New Inn is old. There is an ancient tradition of giving that name to an inn when it replaced an even older establishment that had stood on the same site. Many New Inns date from the reign of Elizabeth I who complained of the lack of suitable places to stay and sup as she toured her kingdom. The Biggleswade inn dates from the 17th century and a makeover in 2016 took it back to its coaching day roots: a micro-brewery was added and food menus were extended. This means today's customers, like those of centuries ago, can enjoy good ale brewed on the premises along with hearty food.

The modest address – 16a Market Square – belies its size, for the large entrance to the side that now leads to a courtyard and beer garden once gave ingress to coaches and horses. Before it was an inn, the building was part of a palace used by the Bishop of Lincoln when he was visiting the town and ministering to his flock. The current convivial hosts were delighted to produce books, including Ken Page's,

In the area

The Shuttleworth Collection
(SG18 9EP; 01767 627927; www.shuttleworth.org) is well signed on the A1 and is based at the Old Warden Aerodrome. It has a large collection of old flying machines and holds regular air displays and events. A number of vintage cars and motorcycles are also on show.

with details of the history of the inn. It's a wonderfully comfortable and comforting place, with beams, standing timbers, open fires, settles, wood-panelling and – a neat touch – stools fashioned from beer casks.

The pub is owned by Greene King and as well as the brewery's beers there are regular guest ales, including Oakham from Peterborough. Add in the house beers and there are ten cask ales to be enjoyed. Not surprisingly, the New Inn Ale House & Kitchen, to give it its new full name, was awarded Pub of the Year status by the local branch of CAMRA in 2016. The food menus are extensive with lunchtime deals and specials. There's a wide range of burgers along with nachos, soup, fish and chips, bangers and mash, butternut squash Wellington, salads and lasagne.

Eaton Socon, Cambridgeshire
(56 miles from London, 367 miles to Edinburgh)

Eaton Socon has an identity crisis. Not only has it been cruelly stripped of its importance as a major stopping place on the Great North Road but it's also been moved from one county to another, from Bedfordshire to Cambridgeshire. To add to the confusion, it may also have been in Huntingdonshire as it's officially part of the major town of St Neots that once resided in that county but has been subsumed into Cambridgeshire.

Charles G Harper in *The Great North Road* describes Eaton Socon as 'once a place of importance ... this is now only a long village of one struggling street.' Important it was. It was a Royal Mail staging post and this stretch of the road played a vital role in coach travel as it had been carefully cut to avoid flooding in winter from the Great River Ouse. A separate loop through St Neots and Huntingdon could be perilous. Harper records that 'two old ladies were on one occasion given a terrible fright, the road being deeply flooded and the water coming into the coach, so that they had to stand on the seats. They quite thought they were going to be drowned.'

The Socon element of the name underscores its importance in medieval times as it comes from soke, meaning a place where justice could be dispensed,

as in the better known Soke of Peterborough. From Tudor times it became a major stop for the Royal Mail but its importance declined with the arrival of the railway in the 19th century and two bypasses built in 1971 and 1985 that cut it off from the A1. Fortunately Eaton Socon's coaching inn has not only survived but thrives and has maintained its historic address.

⑬ White Horse

103 Great North Road, Eaton Socon, PE19 8EL
01480 470853 www.whitehorse-eatonsocon.co.uk

The pub has a striking exterior, with bow windows and a vast creeper covering most of the facade: the creeper is bright

The bar of the White Horse known to Dickens and Pepys; there's even a Dickens Room

green in spring and summer then turns burning red in autumn. The large side entrance that leads to the car park was clearly used by coaches, with stabling for horses.

Inside, a long bar serves several nooks, crannies and bigger seating areas. There's a wealth of ceiling beams, standing timbers, open fires and settles. It must have been a welcoming sight for Nicholas Nickleby and his companions

bound for Dotheboys Hall in the company of headmaster Wackford Squeers. In the novel, Dickens changed the name of the village and recorded that 'At Eton Slocomb there was a good coach-dinner and the five little boys were put to thaw by the fire and regaled with sandwiches'. No doubt Mr Squeers partook of more than just sandwiches. At a later stop, Nicholas and the other boys were left outside the inn while the headmaster went inside to 'stretch his legs'. Nicholas observed: 'After some minutes he returned with his legs thoroughly stretched, if the hue of his nose and a short hiccup afforded any criterion.'

One wood-panelled room at the White Horse is dutifully called after Charles Dickens while a plaque records that Samuel Pepys had also dropped by, as did the Queen of Norway in 1937. The rear of the inn is now given over to a large restaurant where diners can choose from menus offering, among other dishes, soup, pâté, Brie wedges, ham, egg and chips, meat or vegetarian chilli, pie of the day, fish and chips, mushroom stroganoff, salads, steaks, pizzas and burgers. Cask beers include Adnams Ghost Ship, Fuller's London Pride, Sharp's Doom Bar and Wells' Bombardier.

Buckden, Cambridgeshire
(61 miles from London, 362 miles to Edinburgh)

Unlike Eaton Socon, Buckden is just a few yards from the A1 and almost the first two buildings you encounter are coaching inns. In spite of being no more than a large village today, Buckden is of considerable historic importance. It was once owned by the powerful bishops of Lincoln, who built a palace there. It was later renamed Buckden Towers and stands today in large grounds, which are open to visitors. Most of the current buildings date from 1872 but the central tower of the Grade I-listed palace remains. The towers have a turbulent history, due to the marital pursuits of Henry VIII and the short shrift he gave to most of his wives. Catherine of Aragon was held prisoner there from 1533 to 1534 before she was transferred to Kimbolton Castle, where she died.

Henry stayed at Buckden Towers in 1541 with Catherine Howard as they made a tour of the country prior to their wedding. But it was while the couple were staying at Buckden that she was accused of adultery with Thomas Culpepper. As a result, she was tried for treason and beheaded. Today, in more tranquil times, Buckden Towers is a Roman Catholic seminary and place of retreat.

⑭ Lion
High Street, Buckden, PE19 5XA
01480 810313 www.thelionbuckden.com

The Lion dates from 1492 and was originally the kitchen and dining room for the bishops of Lincoln when they visited the town. It's a Grade II-listed building and the tall structure to the right looks identical to a grain hoist in a traditional brewery, which suggests the Lion may once have brewed on the premises.

While the George across the road is now, by its own description, a modern hotel and bistro, the Lion retains all the trappings of a coaching inn. I arrived on a bitterly cold day and was greeted by a blazing fire in the front bar and equally warm greetings from a group of regulars supping pints.

The inn has 14 guest rooms, three of which have four-poster beds, so you can stay in style. It's a pet-friendly place and Fido and Rover may join you if they are well behaved. Meetings can be held in one of the inn's many wood-panelled rooms that have a wealth of beams and standing timbers. There's a large restaurant that serves dishes ranging from ploughman's lunch to antipasti, soup, fish and chips, gnocchi, chicken supreme, burgers and steaks. Cask beers include Adnams, Greene King and Taylor's Landlord.

The Lion at Buckden, tranquil today but in a town with a turbulent past

Brampton, Cambridgeshire
(64 miles from London, 359 miles to Edinburgh)

Brampton has two claims to fame. Samuel Pepys, the celebrated diarist and Secretary to the Admiralty, stayed in the village on many occasions and described it as 'the loveliest and most flowery spot the sun ever beheld'. The Pepys family home, owned by his uncle Robert, at 44 Huntingdon Road, was originally a farmhouse on the estate of Sir Edward Montagu at Hinchingbrooke House. Sir Edward became the first Earl of Sandwich and his descendant, the fourth earl, is best known for inventing the sandwich, described by the *New York Times* – tongue or ham in cheek, no doubt – as England's greatest contribution to gastronomy.

It's claimed that Pepys, alarmed by the prospect of a Dutch invasion of England, buried his gold in the garden of the cottage and when he later recovered the coins he found that some had mysteriously disappeared. The house today is owned by a trust, the Pepys Club, and is not currently open but there are plans to make it accessible to visitors in the future.

⑮ Black Bull
25 Church Road, Brampton, PE28 4PF
01480 457201 www.theblackbull-brampton.co.uk

Pepys drank, ate and even stayed at this 300-year-old inn with its white facade and steeply pitched roof. It's well placed on the main road to Huntingdon and was a convenient resting place for coaches. The Black Bull has retained its heavy beams and a large range offering welcome heat on cold days. The wooden floors are polished and the bar, settles and tables are also built of wood. A yard of ale glass above the bar indicates this is a pub used by serious drinkers who can choose from St Austell Tribute, Sharp's Doom Bar and Taylor's Landlord. The inn has a good reputation for its home-made pies, with a range that includes steak and Stilton, pork and apple, and cheddar, potato and onion. The menu also offers baguettes and jacket potatoes with a choice of fillings.

The bar of the Black Bull where Samuel Pepys regularly ate and drank

Huntingdon, Cambridgeshire
(66 miles from London, 357 miles to Edinburgh)

We will take a slight diversion to visit Huntingdon. It's on the Old North Road, a different route out of London that followed the Roman Ermine Street to Lincoln. Huntingdon is a town of historic importance that also houses two contrasting examples of coaching inns. As the Old North Road joins the Great North Road at Alconbury, just a few miles further north, the diversion is permissible.

Huntingdon is indissolubly linked to Oliver Cromwell. He was born in the town, went to school there and recruited soldiers for his New Model Army there. He went on to defeat Charles I and ushered in a republic that may have been short-lived but introduced a democratic parliament and constitutional monarchy.

The town is ancient, its age shown by a medieval bridge that crosses the Great River Ouse: the bridge was a vital passage for Ermine Street. As a major market town in Huntingdonshire, it became an important stop for both mail carriers and coaches. It was represented in parliament in the 17th century by Oliver Cromwell and more recently by the Conservative Prime Minister John Major.

 George

George Street, Huntingdon, PE29 3AB
01480 432444 www.oldenglishinns.co.uk

The George is palatial and was once even bigger until a fire destroyed a couple of its wings. It's Grade II listed and bestrides the street corner, with a large arched coach entrance leading to a courtyard that also doubles as a beer garden in warm weather. Redesigned in the Georgian period, it was originally a posting house that was bought by Henry Cromwell, Oliver's grandfather. The George was briefly the headquarters of Charles I during the Civil War: was he aware that his nemesis was born there and went to school just over the road? Dick Turpin also stayed at the George, suggesting he was active on the Old North Road as well as the Great North one.

Huntingdon was the first overnight stop on the journey from London and the owners of the George rose to the occasion by employing local tradesmen to improve the facilities with brightly painted walls, wooden panelling and mantels. The inn was a welcome sight for passengers as they alighted from the mud-spattered coaches for much needed food, drink and rest. One of the coachmen on the route was Tom Hennessy who drove the Stamford

George, Huntingdon

Regent, a famous coach, and he became a celebrity of the time. He would strut across the yard of the George, whip aloft, with his caped coat flying in the wind. Sadly, he sank into depression when the railway arrived and deprived him of his livelihood.

The hotel has 27 guest rooms that are highly rated by visitors: the George is part of the Old English Inns group owned by Greene King. This means you will get a rather restricted beer list – IPA and Abbot Ale – and a standardised menu but the plus side is the wealth of well-appointed rooms for drinking, dining and holding meetings. There are impressive pillars that cover timber originals and the walls throughout carry photos, prints and documents detailing the history of both inn and town. The hotel is dog-friendly.

The hotel offers Sunday roasts while weekday menus include soup, Stilton and peppercorn mushrooms, roasted aubergines, black pudding with bubble and squeak, steaks, fish and chips, sea bass, roasted beetroot risotto, sausage and mash, and beer and ale pie. In good weather the George presents Shakespeare productions in the courtyard where a balcony is ideal for staging Romeo and Juliet.

🕧 Falcon

10 Market Hill, Huntingdon, PE29 3NE

01480 457416 www.falconhuntingdon.co.uk

The Falcon is a bird of a different colour to the George. It's believed to be Huntingdon's oldest pub, dating from the 16th century, and is deeply rooted in the town's Civil War history. The inn acted as the recruitment centre where

Courtyard of the George where Shakespeare's plays are staged in summer

Courtyard of the Falcon, once the entrance for coaches, now acting as a beer garden

Cromwell signed up soldiers for his New Model Army that led the long campaign to defeat and execute the king.

The Falcon has been the centre of a more recent campaign. It re-opened in 2014 after a six-year battle by local community groups to save it. They were successful and it once again stands proud on Market Hill, its name emblazoned above an impressive bow window and even more impressive arched gateway that once welcomed coaches and horses. The courtyard is invitingly stacked with beer casks and leads to a large garden.

Inside, the inn is pure delight, with a great oak bar groaning under the weight of 15 handpumps that specialise in cask beers from breweries in the east of England. There are oak settles, beams, standing timbers and open fires. If you clamber up creaking wood stairs to the

In the area

Cromwell Museum (Grammar School Walk, Huntingdon, PE29 3LF; 01480 708008; www. cromwellmuseum.org) – This former almshouse became a school and was where Oliver and his son Richard were educated. It holds around 610 items covering the life and times of Oliver Cromwell, including military clothing worn by the New Model Army, documents and coins from the time of the Civil War and the Protectorate, and portraits and artefacts. The museum is just over the road from the George Hotel and is a 'must visit' for anyone with an interest in English history.

next floor you will find even more beams and a Victorian tea room where you are served by staff dressed in 19th century costumes.

Back downstairs there is good value pub food and a surfeit of ales from the family-owned Elgood's Georgian brewery in Wisbech along with Great Oakley, Nobby's and Potbelly – but the range changes rapidly. A local supping a pint asked me where I was from and when I said St Albans he said ruminatively: 'Agh, that's Hertfordshire, isn't it?' as though it were 200 miles away. 'Just down the Great North Road and turn right at Hatfield,' I said helpfully.

Alconbury, Cambridgeshire
(70 miles from London, 353 miles to Edinburgh)

Alconbury marks the merger of the Great North and Old North roads. It was once a steep climb for coaches but today has the fastest multi-lane stretch of the A1(M) running past RAF Alconbury fighter base. By-passed by the road, Alconbury, formerly in Huntingdonshire, is a large and attractive village with brooks and streams criss-crossed by bridges.

⑱ Manor

20 Chapel Street, Alconbury, PE28 4DY

01480 890423 www.manorhousealconbury.co.uk

The 16th-century Manor is a large and impressive white-painted, bow-windowed inn with a special claim to fame today. In 2015 a large oak tree in the pub garden became diseased. Rather than chop it down, Anne Jones, co-owner of the inn, got in touch with Dennis Heath and David Flemons who run a carvings workshop at Knebworth

House in Hertfordshire. They arrived with chain saws and in just one week had turned the tree into a carved memorial, with faces in the wood and an eagle in flight on top. It has become a major attraction in the area.

Inside the spacious inn there are low

The intricately carved tree at the Manor, Alconbury

The bar of the Manor in Alconbury with a fine timbered ceiling

beams, timbers, settles and open fires at either end of the bar. A brick built bar is supplied with beers from the Greene King range but also serves St Austell Tribute. A separate dining room features the Black Rock Grill where diners can see their chosen dish cooked on volcanic rocks at the table. Other items on the menu include halloumi kebabs, chickpea and sweet potato curry, chilli, and fish and chips. The Manor has six guest rooms.

Stilton
(78 miles from London, 345 miles to Edinburgh)

The story of Stilton village and its coaching inns is inextricably linked to cheese. Stilton is called the King of Cheese by its admirers – myself included – and it's made the small village world famous even though Stilton is now bypassed by the modern A1(M). In a cheese-mad country, there's even a dispute about the origins of Stilton cheese. Some say it was first made at Quenby Hall near Melton Mowbray, which – heaven forfend – is in Leicestershire, not even Cambridgeshire or what used to be Huntingdonshire. The cheese became known as Stilton as it was supplied to inns and pubs in the village and, as its reputation grew, coaches stopped there to refresh passengers and horses before continuing south to deliver cheese to the London aristocracy.

The counter claim, fiercely defended in the village, is that the cheese originated in Stilton itself. The claim has been boosted by the recent discovery of an 18th-century recipe for cream cheese that was made in the village and it's perfectly possible that some of the cheese was aged to become blue. Acting as umpire and adjudicator, I would suggest that, as Melton Mowbray is renowned for its pork pies, it should allow Stilton to have the rights to the cheese.

Stilton is an ancient village that was listed in the Domesday Book in 1086, when it was known as Stichiltone or Sticiltone, meaning 'village at a style or steep ascent'. Both the village and its pubs have been badly affected by changes to transport in the area. The arrival of the railway several miles to the east in the 19th century led to a severe decline in the movement of both goods and people along the Great North Road. The village's problems deepened when it was cut off from the main road when the A1 bypass was opened in 1959.

Revival came in 1962 when Malcolm Moyer, owner of the Bell inn, and Tom McDonald of another local inn, the

Talbot, organised the first cheese rolling race through the village. It's now an annual event, staged every May Day bank holiday and attracts crowds of up to 2,000 people. The contestants, competing in teams of four and often in fancy dress, have to rolls blocks of woods shaped like Stilton cheeses from the Talbot to the Bell. It's a knockout competition and so a mad scramble to the finishing line ensues.

⑲ Bell, Stilton

Great North Road, Stilton, Cambridgeshire, PE7 3RA Tel 01733 241066 www.thebellstilton.co.uk

The Bell, with its enormous hanging sign and honey-coloured buildings, is superb, one of the finest old coaching inns on

The eagerly fought Stilton cheese rolling competition

Stilton making

Fresh milk is poured into open vats and acid-forming bacteria and rennet – a clotting agent – are added, along with *penicillium roqueforti*: blue mould spores named after another famous blue cheese, Roquefort. Once the curds have formed, the whey is removed and the curds are allowed to drain overnight. The mixture is placed in cylindrical moulds and after nine to twelve weeks the crusts are pierced with stainless steel needles to allow air into the core. Blue cheese making has much in common with Belgian Lambic and Gueuze beers, fermented with wild yeasts in the air.

Modern Stilton has been cleaned up. In 1722, in *A Tour thro' the Whole Island of Great Britain*, Daniel Defoe wrote:

'We passed through Stilton, a town famous for its cheese, which is called our English Parmesan, and brought to the table with mites or maggots round it, so thick that they bring a spoon with them for you to eat the mites as you do the cheese.'

Stilton has an *appellation* or protected status from the European Union. The cheese can be made only in the counties of Derbyshire, Leicestershire and Nottinghamshire and the approved manufacturers are Colston Bassett, Cropwell Bishop, Long Clawson, Pikehall and Saxelbye. Stilton village's application to also have protected status was rejected in 2013 but the local Member of Parliament is campaigning to have the ruling overthrown.

the Great North Road. It has sweeping staircases, open fires, inglenooks and massively beamed rooms. It dates from 1500 and could be even earlier. It was rebuilt in 1642, a significant date as it's also the year the English Civil War started, with Oliver Cromwell based in Huntingdon just 12 miles away: the date is marked on the southern gable of the inn. The inn was built of limestone, with slates of Collyweston stone, and when it was restored in 1990 the architect kept to the original plans lodged in the Bodleian Library in Oxford. As a result, it has retained its mullioned windows, imposing rear courtyard and central carriageway. The position of the carriage entrance is unusual as they are more usually sited to the side of the inn. The Bell's fame and prosperity is due to its role first as a posting inn and then as a coach stop. Stilton was such an important point for the delivery of mail that local innkeepers were prepared to

pay £40 – a considerable sum at the time – to become the local postmaster. When Stilton became a major posting stage from the 17th century, the village had 14 inns that served a population of just 500. Inevitably, there's a Dick Turpin connection. It's alleged that he hid for nine weeks in the Bell while he was being hunted by officers of the law. When they raided the Bell, Turpin, it's claimed, threw open the window of his room, jumped on to the ever-faithful Black Bess and galloped off up the Great North Road.

A more recent visitor was a British prime minister who stayed the night with a lady who was not his wife: my lips are sealed.

But without doubt the most important resident of the Bell was the innkeeper Cooper Thornhill, the landlord from 1730 to 1759. He discovered blue cheese when he visited Quenby Hall and then ensured it was served every day at the Bell. His forename Cooper suggests he may also have been a cask maker and even brewed ale at the Bell.

The Bell closed when the village was cut off by the A1 bypass, and a number of other businesses in the village failed at the same time. But happily the Bell is

Central carriageway and rear courtyard at the Bell, Stilton

now thriving once more and is a popular wedding venue. It has meeting places and 22 guest rooms, some with four-poster beds. There is an evening restaurant and also a bistro and bar where full meals and snacks are served lunchtime and evening. The beers on offer in the large, beamed and mullioned bar include Greene King IPA and 1799 and two changing guest beers, often one from Oakham Ales in nearby Peterborough. Meals can conclude with a Stilton platter that offers samples of all the accredited versions of the cheese.

Famous guests *John Churchill (1st Duke of Marlborough), Daniel Defoe (writer), Lord Byron (poet), Dave Clark (musician) and Freddie Mercury (singer). Freddie Mercury stayed at the Bell while he was filming the music video for Breakthru on the nearby Nene Valley steam train line.*

Wansford, Cambridgeshire
(85 miles from London, 338 miles to Edinburgh)

The Haycock, with its attractive gold-coloured buildings, stands alongside the modern A1 and draws you into the fascinating village of Wansford. It's also known as Wansford-in-England as the result of a tale about a local man who, taken with drink, fell asleep on a hay rick and woke to find himself floating down the River Nene. He saw a man on the river bank and called out: 'Where am I?' When he was told Wansford, he asked: 'Is that Wansford in England?'

⓴ Haycock Hotel

Wansford, Cambridgeshire PE8 6JA 01780 782223
www.macdonaldhotels.co.uk/haycock

This sumptuous feast of an inn, standing alongside the River Nene, has hosted – among many other famous people – Elizabeth I and Mary, Queen of Scots. Elizabeth was en route to visit Lord Burghley in Stamford while poor Mary suffered a rougher fate: she went on from Wansford to Fotheringay Castle where she was executed for treason. She is one of several ghouls that haunt the inn, which organises regular ghost hunts. I was shown the room where Elizabeth stayed and I trust she enjoyed the multi-channel television at the foot of her four-poster bed.

You could spend hours at the Haycock sitting and staring in wonder at the splendours offered by the inn. Most of the current building dates from 1632 but an inn has stood on the site for longer still. As well as 48 guest rooms, it has a wealth of rooms set aside for dining, afternoon tea, relaxing or holding meetings. The old Coach House can seat no fewer than 250 people. The rooms are decorated with portraits and scenes of the inn and the village spanning several centuries.

The large courtyard is a delightful place to sit in good weather while a pétanque court offers undemanding exercise: the adjacent cricket pitch occasionally disappears under water when the Nene floods.

The garden at the Haycock that offers pétanque and, occasionally, underwater cricket

The Haycock has a fine reputation for its meals, prepared by chef Luke Holland: his creations can be enjoyed in several dining rooms including the Orchard Restaurant. Dishes include scallops, moules, white bean and celeriac soup, bruschetta, chicken breast, sea bass, butternut squash risotto, salad niçoise, venison, and wild mushroom fettucine. The hotel welcomes well-behaved pets. There is just one changing cask beer in the bar: you will find greater choice in the Paper Mills, London Road, which specialises in beers from regional independent breweries.

On the area

Nene Valley Steam Railway (Wansford Station, Old Great North Road, Stibbington, PE8 6LR; 01780 784444; www.nvr.org) – A thriving heritage railway which runs regular steam trains and occasional diesel services.

Peterborough CAMRA beer festival (www.peterborough-camra. org.uk) – Held in August, this is second in size only to the Great British Beer Festival in London.

One of the many sumptuous rooms for residents at the Haycock

Ermine Street: to Gumster and back

The A1 and A1(M) have little in common with the Great North Road, save for those towns and villages, now bypassed by the modern road, where we can still catch a glimpse of the old road, Welwyn being a good example. The recently expanded stretch of the A1(M) in the Alconbury area is more like an American highway and it's a relief to spot the turn for Stilton and the tranquillity offered by the Bell Inn.

But it's possible to get the feel for one of the old coaching routes by picking up the Old North Road, based on the Roman Ermine Street. It started in London, like the Great North Road, but went from Shoreditch to Stamford Hill and on to Ware and Royston in Hertfordshire. It then crossed Cambridgeshire until it reached Godmanchester and Huntingdon, where it joined the Great North Road at Alconbury.

The stretch from Royston – where I picked it up – to Godmanchester is now officially the A1198 but street names and signs still refer to Ermine Street and there are milestones every step of the way. Except for two minor deviations to bypass modern industrial and housing estates, the road runs straight as a die all the way to Godmanchester. It passes through attractive villages, some with thatched cottages, and the vast Wimpole Hall estate.

Wimpole Hall was a moated manor house at the time of the Domesday Book in 1066 and grew in stately size to cover vast acres of parkland and a farm but its upkeep ruined a series of nobles. It was rescued by the writer Rudyard Kipling's family who eventually bequeathed it to the National Trust.

The Hardwicke Arms, Arrington, in 1887

Close to the estate, and with the splendid address of 96 Ermine Street, Arrington, you will find the Hardwicke Arms, a striking, creeper-clad old coaching inn, standing proud by the side of the historic road. It dates from the 13th century but the building we see today is largely 18th century in design. Outbuildings at the rear were once stables and the inn was clearly an important stop for coaches and travellers on the long haul out of London. Inside there's an almost endless series of inter-linked rooms, with heavy beams, wood panelling and open fires. The bar is cosy and popular with locals while there's a large dining room. Accommodation, in the finest traditions of coaching inns, is still available.

Pressing on, the road takes you through a series of places with Caxton in the name: Caxton, Caxton End and, alarmingly, Caxton Gibbet. There's no connection with William Caxton, inventor of the first printing press in the 15th century, who came from Kent. Caxton itself was once an important stage on the coach route but fell from the grace when coaching came to an end. A traveller in 1863 described it as 'a small rambling village, which looked as if it had not shaved and washed its face, and put on a clean shirt for a shocking length of time'.

Equally shocking, the gibbet is a stark reminder of the short shrift given to highwaymen. William Cole, an antiquarian from Cambridge, wrote: 'Around 1753 or 1754 the son of Mrs Gatward being convicted of robbing the Mail was hanged in chains on the Great Road. I saw him hanging in a scarlet coat after he had hung for 2 or 4 months. It is supposed that the screw was filed which supported him and that he fell in the first high wind after.'

It's a relief to leave this area and arrive in Godmanchester. It's a small town of historic importance. It was a Roman site called Durovigutum and was a key cross roads for the invaders, with Ermine Street meeting the Via Devana from Cambridge and a military road from Sandy in Bedfordshire, while the Great River Ouse, which dominates the town, was an important waterway.

The name of the town comes from a tribal chief called Godmund. Godmanchester is a mouthful and difficult to pronounce, and locals get round the problem by calling it Gumster.

It's a magical place, like entering a Hansel and Gretel fairy tale. The streets are packed with unspoilt half-timbered black and white houses, with a few splendid Georgian buildings in between. The tree-lined Ouse seems as wide as the Thames while the Chinese Bridge that crosses a mill stream alongside the river is one the town's best-known features. The original bridge was built in 1827 when an architectural style known as Chinese Chippendale was popular. It fell into disrepair and was replaced by a replica in 1827.

Even though Godmanchester is very close to Huntingdon, it was an important coaching stop in its own right and still

has two fine inns from that period. The Black Bull stands at 32 Post Road, emphasising the important role played by mail coaches. In spite of its name, it's a white-faced building with a large function room to one side and other buildings at the rear that were once stables. Inside there are large rooms with heavy beamed ceilings, standing timbers and in the dining area a large and welcoming inglenook with a blazing fire. The stately inn dates from the 17th century but is now mainly 18th century in design. It's comforting to find that it's run today by the splendidly named Paul and Karen Beer who have selected

Adnams Southwold Bitter for the bar along with – a neat touch – Theakston's Black Bull. Accommodation is available. The White Hart, 2 Cambridge Road, is 15th century and shows it with its half-timbered facade and a beamed and wood-panelled interior. It serves Fuller's London Pride and Greene King IPA and it has a good local following for its imaginative menus.

Godmanchester has no fewer than 130 listed buildings. It's a breathtaking small town, a living and breathing example of coaching's glorious past. In short, do go to Gumster!

3

Stamford to Retford

A1 (M)

Doncaster

Retford
(Barnby Moor)
24 Olde Bell

Olde Bell, Barnby Moor

A1

Newark
23 Prince Regent

Grantham
22 Angel & Royal

A1

Angel & Royal, Grantham

Stamford
21 George

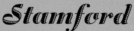
Wansford

A1 (M)

George, Stamford

*L*ondon and the Home Counties recede into the distance. The road now takes us into the Midlands, the Heart of England, and to some of the most handsome towns along the entire route. History is all around: Sherwood Forest with its Robin Hood connections and some of the bloodiest battles of the Wars of the Roses and the Civil War. And in pride of place there are some peerless old coaching inns.

Stamford, Lincolnshire
(93 miles from London, 330 miles to Edinburgh)

With no fewer than 600 listed buildings, Stamford with its honey-coloured limestone and half-timbered buildings draws television and film crews like a magnet: both *Middlemarch* and *Pride and Prejudice* have been filmed there in recent years. It's arguably the finest preserved town in England, and was voted in 2013 by the *Sunday Times* as the best place to live in the country. Its early wealth was based on the wool trade, the riches endowing many fine churches and Stamford School, an acclaimed seat of learning that dates from 1532. Remarkably, Stamford survived 1461 when it was the scene of a fierce battle during the Wars of the Roses that destroyed many of its buildings.

The town rose again and in later centuries fine Georgian and Regency houses added to its stunning beauty. Its most famous estate, on the edge of town and alongside the River Welland, is Burghley House. It was built by Sir William Cecil, later Lord Burghley, one of Elizabeth I's most powerful and trusted advisors: she often visited the house, which today is the ancestral home of the Marquess of Exeter. Stamford also has the most famous of all the old coaching inns on the Great North Road: the George.

㉑ George
71 St Martin's, Stamford, PE9 2LB 01780 750750
www.georgehotelofstamford.com

The George, with its 'gallows' sign stretching imperiously across the road, can boast a long list of famous people that have stayed there. They include Charles I, William III, the King of Denmark and the Duke of Cumberland – Butcher Cumberland – who caroused with his supporters after brutally

suppressing the Scots at Culloden. Sir Walter Scott was a regular guest and wrote that the view of Stamford from St Martins where the inn stands 'was the finest twixt Edinburgh and London'.

And yet for all its grandeur and royal connections, the George is not pompous. Pride of place in the entrance hall is given to a suitably large portrait of Daniel Lambert (1770-1809), a customer who earned the reputation of being England's fattest man: the inn also displays the walking stick he used to help him manoeuvre his giant frame. Lambert, from Leicester, increased weight at such an alarming rate that he became wealthy by putting himself on public display in London. When he died in Stamford, he weighed 52 stone 11lb (335 kilograms). It took 20 men to move his coffin from the George to the cemetery at St Martin's Church: the coffin was on wheels as it couldn't be carried and measured 112 square feet (10.4 square metres). The reasons for Lambert's extraordinary size are unknown: apparently he did not eat excessively and he claimed he 'abstained from alcohol'. As well as his portrait, Lambert is commemorated by a room named in his honour: it is suitably spacious.

The George was once a small, humble inn and owes its present

The courtyard at the George: a wonderful place to dine al fresco in the warmer weather

The oak-panelled dining room at the George.

𝒪n the area

Burghley House (PE9 3JY; 01780
752451; www.burghley.co.uk) – One
of the grandest houses of Elizabethan
England. The house is surrounded by
a deer park and gardens largely
redesigned by 'Capability' Brown in
the 18th century. The annual Burghley
Horse Trials are held in the grounds
at the end of August.

Melbourn Bros brewery (22 All
Saints' Street, Stamford, PE9 2PA;
01780 752186; www.allsaintsbrewery.
co.uk) – This Grade II-listed building
opened in 1825, closed in the 20th
century but reopened in 1994 when
it was bought by Samuel Smith's of
Tadcaster in Yorkshire. The brewery
has antique steam-powered brewing
equipment and makes a range of
organic fruit beers. Brewery tours are
available and it has a pub on site.

imposing size and sumptuous
architecture to the age of coaching. It
stands on the site of the House of the
Holy Sepulchre, a monastic hospice
where the Knights of St John of
Jerusalem were entertained before
travelling on to fight in the Crusades. A
church and an almshouse, the Hospital
of St John and St Thomas, also stood on
the site. Some of the thick exterior walls
of the hospice are now inside the

present building while the tranquil
church garden can be enjoyed today by
visitors to the George. A gnarled old
mulberry bush in the gardens dates from
the reign of James I: some historians
place it even earlier during the time of
Elizabeth I.

The inn developed a central role in
the life of Stamford. In the 15th century,
its proprietor, John Dickens, was an
alderman in the town and his daughter
Alice's marriage to David Cissell
launched one of the most powerful
aristocratic families in England. Cissell's
son Richard was the father of William
Cecil – note the change of spelling – the
first Lord Burghley. It was Lord Burghley
who rebuilt the George in 1597 and his
coat of arms is engraved above the front
entrance to the inn. The mullioned
latticed windows in the upper storey
above the main block root the building
firmly in the Elizabethan period.

The George came to its present pomp
and glory in the 18th century. The front
of the inn was rebuilt and the famous
gallows sign was erected to welcome
passengers as their coaches rumbled
along St Martin's. The majestically
panelled York and London rooms pay
homage to the astonishing amount of
coach business conducted by the inn: it
boasted '20 up and 20 down' as it
handled 40 coaches a day going to and
from London and York.

Lovingly maintained, the George
oozes antiquity. As well as wood
panelling, there are flagged floors,

The George's biggest customer, Daniel Lambert

The Ram Jam

There's a sad and mournful site on the stretch of the Great North Road between Stamford and Grantham: the boarded-up Ram Jam Inn at Stretton, near Oakham. It was once a much used coaching inn but it closed in 2013 and is up for sale with a price of £500,000: there are no plans to reopen it as a pub.

The inn was originally called the Winchelsea Arms but was renamed as a result of an alleged incident involving Dick Turpin. He lodged at the inn for some time but avoided paying his bill by ramming the thumbs of the landlady, Mrs Spring, into the two holes – the bung and the spile – in a cask of ale. She was trapped and Turpin made good his escape. A variation on the story is that another unnamed highwayman performed the trick on the landlord so he could seduce his wife. Whatever the truth of these tales, the name stuck.

In more recent decades, the Ram Jam became a popular stopping place on the road for musical groups on their way to and from gigs: the soul singer Geno Washington named his backing group the Ram Jam Band following a visit to the inn in the 1960s.

beams, standing timbers and vast fireplaces: imagine frozen coach travellers warming themselves by the log fires as they drank strong and restorative potions. Luxurious accommodation is available today in 45 guest rooms. Meals and afternoon tea are served in several wood-panelled reception rooms, with beer and snacks in the York Bar: there are three resident chefs. Cask beers include Adnams Southwold Bitter, Fuller's London Pride and Grainstore Triple B. A range of fine wines is stored in vaults that date back to the earliest days of the inn.

Shuttered and forlorn: the Ram Jam Inn

Grantham, Lincolnshire
(113 miles from London, 310 miles to Edinburgh)

Grantham is an ancient market town with several claims to fame. Oliver Cromwell won a major battle of the Civil War close by at Gonerby Moor. The turmoil caused by the war destroyed the Eleanor Cross in the town that had been erected in 1290. It commemorated the passage through the town of the funeral cortege of Eleanor of Castile, en route for Westminster Abbey in London. Her husband, King Edward I, accompanied the cortege.

Sir Isaac Newton (1642-1726) has fared better. The physicist and mathematician, recognised as one of the greatest scientific minds of all time, was born in neighbouring Woolsthorpe and educated at King's School in Grantham. There's an impressive statue celebrating his work in the town and there's even a pub named in his honour at 7 High Street.

Grantham's most famous modern citizen remains a divisive figure. Margaret Thatcher, Britain's first woman prime minister, elected in 1979, was born in the town where her father ran a grocer's shop. Her legacy remains so potent, even after her death in 2013, that plans to erect a statue of her have been fiercely opposed. Even a modest bust in the Grantham Museum met with complaints before it finally went on show.

㉒ Angel & Royal

High Street, Grantham, NG31 6PN
01476 565816 www.angelandroyal.co.uk

The Angel & Royal is believed to be the oldest of all the surviving coaching inns in Britain. It's Grade I listed and was described by Sir Nikolaus Pevsner, the acclaimed architectural historian, as one of the most impressive pre-Reformation inns left standing. The history is awe-inspiring. The cellars and part of the foundations date back to the ninth century when it was a humble monks' dwelling. In 1203, a hostel was built on the site for the Knights Templar, the religious, quasi-military charitable organisation that sent members to fight in the Crusades and became one of the most powerful bodies in Europe until it was dissolved by Papal decree. The Templars were evicted from the hostel in 1308 by the Sheriff of Lincolnshire and it became an inn to accommodate travellers on the Ermine Way.

The present facade of the Angel dates from 1415 and the inn was further extended in the 14th and 15th centuries as more and more vehicles used the Ermine Way and Great North Road. The Angel has welcomed an impressive list of celebrities over the centuries, including King John of Magna Carta fame. Edward III and his wife Philippa of Hainault stayed twice in the 14th century, their presence marked by two corbels – plaster mouldings – of their heads above the entrance. Oliver Cromwell held court here following the

battle of Gonerby Moor in 1643 and wrote: 'God hath given us, this evening, a glorious victory over our enemies.' The most fateful event took place at the Angel in 1483 when Richard III, sitting in the vast Chambre de Roi on the first floor, sent for the Great Seal in order to sign the warrant for the execution of Henry Stafford, the Duke of Buckingham, for high treason. The room, with its mullioned windows, beams and open fireplaces, is used as a restaurant today: its French name is a reminder that the House of Plantagenet, which lost power when Richard was killed at Bosworth, was originally from France and French was the language used at court. Copies of the warrant are displayed at the inn: the original is held at the British Museum in London.

The inn remained a popular resting place for royalty. In 1866, the Prince of Wales, later Edward VII, stayed here and as a result it took on the current name of Angel & Royal. There is still so much to enchant and regale the modern traveller, including the great arched entrance that once allowed coaches to disembark their travellers and feed and rest the horses in the stables at the rear. In recent years a medieval fireplace measuring nine feet wide by six feet high (2.74 metres by 1.83 metres) was discovered behind a wall and it's likely the inn has many other treasures hidden from view.

It has 32 rooms for guests and several restaurants, including the King's Room and Bertie's Bistro, the latter named after

The hustle and bustle of the market place in Grantham in 1836 with the Angel & Royal in the centre

Edward VII. Dishes may include French onion soup, smoked salmon, Brie, tomato and rocket tortellini, lamb chop, salmon Wellington stuffed with spinach and ricotta, and tandoori paneer vegetarian curry. The bar serves cask beers from Oldershaw's brewery in Grantham: one beer is called Newton's Drop, a reference to the tale that Isaac Newton was inspired to develop his laws of gravity when he saw an apple fall from a tree.

On the area

Grantham Museum (St Peter's Hill, NG31 6PY; 01476 568783; www.granthammuseum.org.uk) – Local museum with exhibitions on Sir Isaac Newton, Margaret Thatcher and the Dambusters.

St Wulfram's Church (Church Street, Grantham) – Grade I listed with one of the finest steeples in England.

Newark, Nottinghamshire

(127 miles from London, 296 miles to Edinburgh)

It's a short, straight journey along the Great North Road from Grantham to Newark but, as we exchange Lincolnshire for Nottinghamshire, we travel along what used to be Gonerby Hill, once one of the most demanding stretches of the road. The seemingly unending rise of the hill put a terrible strain on horses and its undulations created excellent hideouts for highwaymen. As the coaches creaked and rattled slowly up the hill, it was easy for 'the Gentlemen of the Road', guns raised menacingly, to stop them and rob their passengers. But their activities were not without risk: a gibbet was raised alongside the road and any highwayman caught was given short shrift. Gonerby Hill became infamous from London to Edinburgh as the place where travellers might come across the grisly sight of a body dangling from the gallows.

There were other dangers on this part of the road created by the weather. In *Nicholas Nickleby*, Dickens records: 'Nicholas, who had been asleep for a short time, was suddenly roused by a violent jerk which nearly threw him from his seat. Grasping the rail, he found that the coach had sunk greatly on one side, though it was still dragged forward by the horses; and while – confused by the plunging and the loud screams of the

lady inside – he hesitated for an instant whether to jump off or not, the vehicle turned easily over, and relieved him from all further uncertainty by flinging him into the road.' There were no serious injuries and eventually the coach was righted and the passengers went on to the warmth and comfort of an inn in Newark.

The road has long since been flattened and landscaped and modern travellers can journey at ease as we enter Robin Hood country, with Sherwood Forest, the Trent Valley and the Vale of Belvoir. The Trent Valley is where the waters played an important role in the development of pale ale brewing in the 19th century, and the Vale of Belvoir – pronounced Beaver – holds the ancestral home of the Dukes of Rutland at Belvoir Castle.

Newark-on-Trent is an ancient market town dating back to Roman times. Its early wealth was based on the wool and cloth trade and it has retained a large and bustling market in the town centre. But its main claim to fame is that it was possibly the most-fought over town in the Civil War: the story is brilliantly told in the Civil War Centre on Appletongate. Newark was besieged by Cromwell's troops in 1644 and was relieved by Prince Rupert, Charles I's nephew, in a

In the area

National Civil War Centre
(14 Appletongate, Newark,
NG24 1JY; 01636 655765;
www.nationalcivilwarcentre.com)
Newark Castle and Gardens
(Castle Gate, NG24 1BG;
01636 650000;
www.newark-sherwooddc.gov.uk) –
Founded in the 12th century by the
Bishop of Lincoln, the castle was
partly destroyed in 1646 at the end
of the Civil War. Visitors can tour
the castle's towers and dungeons in
the summer months.

battle known as the Relief of Newark.
But the royalist victory was short lived.
The town was besieged again by
parliamentary forces between November
1845 and May 1846. The citizens suffered
terribly and were almost starved to
death. Charles's troops eventually
surrendered and the king himself gave
up the fight in Oxford.

Prince Rupert's role is not forgotten.
Most of the old coaching inns around
the market place, including the Olde
White Hart where Nicholas Nickleby
stayed, have disappeared. The Clinton
Arms, a major building on Market Place,
closed in 1990. Lord Byron stayed there
and it was the political headquarters of
William Gladstone, the British prime
minister, who was Newark's MP between

1832 and 1841. But the beer 'relief of
Newark' is still at hand.

㉓ Prince Rupert

46 Stodman Street, Newark, NG24 1AW
01636 918121 www.kneadpubs.co.uk

Stodman Street is a short, narrow road
off the Market Place. The Prince Rupert
stands out with its jettied half-timbered
and brick facade that opens on to a
narrow corridor leading to the bar. Most
customers have to bend as the beamed
ceilings are very low, a reminder that
our forebears were considerably shorter.
This stupendous old tavern has small
rooms to left and right, all with beams,
standing timbers, high-back settles, and
wood and flagstone floors. It dates from
1452 and is built in a style known as
Wealden that originated in Kent. It was
owned by a rich merchant before
becoming an inn and it provided
accommodation and stabling for Prince
Rupert's troops.

In the 20th century it was known as
the Woolpack and was owned by the
Yorkshire brewer John Smith of
Tadcaster, which bought Hole's brewery
in Newark. The pub closed in 2010 but it
was bought by a local farmer, Michael
Philby, who spent several years and a lot
of money restoring what had become a
rather seedy pub to its former glory. A
conservatory has been added and is a
beer lovers' paradise with an array of
brewery memorabilia. Old posters,
enamel signs and mirrors recall the
living and the dead: Bass, Guinness,

Fremlin, Hammerton's Stout from London, Hole's, Warwick & Richardson and Watney, to name just a few. There's even a plaque advertising Andrew's Liver Salts for those who have imbibed too deeply. The breweriana spills over into a courtyard used for eating and drinking.

If you manage to scramble up narrow, winding stairs to the first floor you will find further beamed rooms set aside for the necessary business of eating and drinking. The range of beers is ever-changing but you may find Acorn IPA, North Riding and Oakham: but be prepared to be surprised and delighted. The food, served all day, is equally imaginative. The Prince Rupert specialises in pizza for consumption in the inn or for takeaway but you can also gorge on a range of other dishes, including venison ragu, falafel burger, seafood stew, beef brisket, shepherd's pie and ciabatta sandwiches. The inn hosts regular live music and other events. Not to be missed.

The heavily beamed bar at the Prince Rupert serves an ever-changing range of beers

Retford, Nottinghamshire
(152 miles from London, 271 miles to Edinburgh)

In *Along the Great North Road*, published in 1939, William C Boswell said 'There's something rather tragic about the White Hart'. He was referring to the 'soulless modernisation' of Retford's major coaching inn on the corner of the main square. What would he think in recent years when part of the inn was a restaurant called Clockwork Molly's? Following a series of closures and re-openings, there's now a pub on site but it's a sad fall from grace. It was once a major posting house on the Great North Road. Its most famous post boy was John Blagg who worked at the White Hart for 45 years and once rode from Retford to York and back in one day, a distance of 110 miles.

It's only five miles to our next inn in the hamlet of Barnby Moor. In spite of its isolation and bleak terrain, it was a major and popular halt on the road. Laurence Sterne, the author of *Tristram Shandy*, regarded as the first English novel, lived in Yorkshire and when travelling south to London would make a point of heading for Barnby Moor as an overnight stop. Many others have followed in his footsteps.

24 Olde Bell

Great North Road (A638), Barnby Moor, Retford, DN22 8QS 01777 705121
www.yeoldebell-hotel.co.uk

A large model of a racing horse in the Olde Bell highlights its long connections with racing, with Doncaster racecourse not far off, famous for the St Leger. The landlord from 1800 to 1842 was George

The Lady Jane Suite at Ye Olde Bell

Clarke, a keen horse breeder and farmer. He provided stabling for 120 horses as the inn became a popular stop for coach travellers. Clarke also tackled the unrest among agricultural labourers in the 1830s in what were known as the Swing Riots. The labourers set fire to hay ricks and when Clarke heard of rick burning near the inn he set out with post boys and stable hands to apprehend the culprits. Two were caught, hiding in a ditch, and were tried, prosecuted and – poor wretches – transported to Australia.

The Bell is elegant and charming, with large archways leading from room to room, heavy beams, settles, open fires,

The St Leger Bistro at Ye Olde Bell

wood panelling, mullioned windows and casement clocks. The wood panels in the Bradgate Suite came from Bradgate House in Leicestershire, the home of Lady Jane Grey who was queen for just nine days before Queen Mary had her executed in 1554. There are claims that Lady Jane haunts the room. In happier times, Princess Victoria, later the queen, stayed at the Bell in 1835 while she was travelling with her mother, the Duchess of Kent, to a music festival in York. Their rooms are now called the Victoria Suite.

In the modern age, the Bell was an official stop for the Monte Carlo rally and many motoring events, including vintage car rallies, still take place there. Scenes for a film version of JB Priestley's *The Good Companions* were shot at the inn.

The roll call of celebrities who have stayed is impressive. They include Bing Crosby, who used it as a base for Doncaster racecourse, prime ministers Harold Wilson and Edward Heath, Charlie Chaplin, Alec Guinness, Shirley Bassey, and Oliver Reed. No doubt the last named headed for the bar, with its high-back settles and a good range of beers, which included Black Sheep, Draught Bass, Taylor Landlord and a local beer from Pheasantry on my visit.

The Bell has more than 50 guest rooms, including some in the former stable block. Excellent food is served in both the main restaurant and a bistro. Crank up the Lagonda and go.

The Monte Carlo rally at Ye Olde Bell in 1959

Highwaymen

The most famous – or infamous – highwayman who was active along the Great North Road during the coaching period was Richard or Dick Turpin. His exploits are the stuff of legends: books, plays and films have featured him and many have turned him into an almost heroic figure. In real life, he was a robber and a killer.

Most importantly, he did not ride from London to York overnight, a journey of around 200 miles, on his faithful horse Black Bess. It was pure fiction, written by a Victorian novelist William Harrison Ainsworth in 1834 almost 100 years after Turpin's death.

Highwaymen flourished from around 1660 until the late 18th and early 19th centuries. They were distinct from other robbers, such as footpads, as they operated on horseback. Post boys and coaches were tempting bait for highwaymen as many travellers carried money in the form of gold and could be held up at gunpoint with the famous cry of 'Stand and Deliver'. The robbers were able to flourish as the country was lawless, there was no proper police force and roads were open and woods alongside acted as convenient hiding places.

The historian Roy Porter described, in 1982, the period and the activities of the highwaymen as a hallmark of public life: 'From the rough house of the crowds to the dragoons' musket volley, violence was as English as plum pudding. Force was used not just criminally, but as a matter of routine to achieve social and political goals, smudging hard-and-fast distinctions between the worlds of criminality and politics...Highwaymen were romanticised, with a hidden irony, as "gentlemen of the road".

They robbed without distinction, the poor being as likely to lose their goods and small amounts of money as the rich. Highwaymen operated quite openly, often in broad daylight. The 18th-century politician Horace Walpole was shot at in Hyde Park in central London and commented: 'One is forced to travel, even at noon, as if one was going to battle'. Lord North, the prime minister, said in 1774: 'I was robbed last night as I expected, our loss was not great, but as the postilion [coach driver] did not stop immediately one of the two highwaymen fired at him.' This happened in Gunnersbury Lane in west London, proving that the capital city was not a

Dick Turpin

safe place. In fact, Finchley Common in north London, on the Great North Road, was a notorious area for highwaymen, with many reports of violent attacks on coaches and travellers on horseback.

As well as Dick Turpin, other famous highwaymen of the period included James Hind, a former Cavalier; the French-born, so-called 'gentleman highwayman' Claude du Vall; John Nevison; Sixteen String Jack; William Plunkett and James MacLaine. Many took up robbery as a result of losing their army roles after the English Civil War and the wars with France: Hind and du Vall came from relatively well-to-do

backgrounds. The famous 1945 British film *The Wicked Lady*, in which Margaret Lockwood played a nobleman's wife who became a highway woman, was not, perhaps, wide of the mark, as it was claimed to be based on a real life character, Lady Barbara Skelton. There's a Wicked Lady pub between St Albans and Wheathampstead in Hertfordshire close to the area where she operated on Nomansland Common.

Most highwaymen ended up on the gallows as the penalty for robbery and horse stealing was hanging. This was the case with Dick Turpin (1705-1739). As a result of his association with the

The Spaniards is one of the many inns where it's claimed Turpin operated from

poacher and later joined the notorious Essex Gang that carried out violent robberies in the county. Many of them were eventually caught and hanged at Tyburn, with their bodies put on display on gibbets on Edgware Road.

Turpin turned to the highway and travelled the Great North Road and other routes in search of booty. He was implicated in the murder of a man in Whitechapel, east London, and then went on to kill the servant of a keeper in Epping Forest on the Essex-London border. To escape arrest, he moved to Yorkshire and lived under the name of John Palmer. He was arrested under that name for horse stealing and was taken to York Castle. When he wrote to his brother-in-law, his handwriting was

Spaniards inn in north London, it's a common mistake to think Turpin came from Hampstead. In fact, he was born in Hempstead in Essex in another hostelry, the Blue Bell Inn. He became a deer

The gravestone that reputedly marks the spot where Turpin is buried in St George's graveyard, York

Claude Duval (aka du Vall, the so-called 'gentleman highwayman') by Willian Powell Frith, 1860

recognised and he was unmasked as Dick Turpin. He was put on trial, found guilty of horse stealing and hanged on 7th April 1739 at Knavesmire, also known as 'York Tyburn' after the original Tyburn gallows in London. His body was taken to the Blue Boar Inn in Castlegate (see page 123) before being buried in the graveyard of St George's Church in Fishergate.

Highway robbery went into rapid decline as a result of armed tollgates and turnpikes being erected on the Great North Road and other major highways. A police force was created in London and patrolled such dangerous areas as Finchley Common while the replacement of gold coins by traceable bank notes made robbery less profitable. And the arrival of the steam train put a final end to the practice. Even Dick Turpin would have found it difficult to hold up a train.

4

Doncaster to *Northallerton*

Darlington

Northallerton

36 Black Bull
35 Golden Lion

A684   A168

Thirsk
A61

34 Three Tuns
33 Golden Fleece

Three Tuns, Thirsk

Boroughbridge

32 Black Bull
31 Crown Hotel

B1224

Wetherby

30 Swan & Talbot

York

A64

29 Olde Starre
28 Old White Swan
27 Golden Fleece
26 Blue Boar

Ferrybridge

Doncaster

25 Red Lion

Red Lion, Doncaster

A1 (M)

Retford

*Y*orkshire marked the end of the Great North Road before it was extended further north. London to York was the intention of the early road builders and coaching inns were either built or developed from simple posting houses to meet the needs of travellers. Doncaster, Ferrybridge, Wetherby and finally York itself became important coach stops and welcomed not only royalty and aristocracy but also those attending the many horse racing courses that developed in God's Own County.

Doncaster, South Yorkshire

(167 miles from London, 256 miles to Edinburgh)

Writing in 1939 in *Along the Great North Road,* William C Boswell said witheringly of Doncaster that 'Not much of the ancient town is left to tempt one to linger' and he hurried on his testy way to York. He did stay long enough to point out that, as the traveller crosses the quietly flowing River Don, the town marks an important historic divide: the original Great North Road goes on its way to York while the modern version, the A1(M), keeps its distance from the capital and roars off towards the cooling towers of Ferrybridge power station and on to Wetherby and Boroughbridge.

What would Boswell – William C, that is, not his illustrious forebear – make of Doncaster in the 21st century? A vast, multi-storey shopping centre and car park loom over the town. Its importance

as a Roman camp and an Anglo-Saxon fortress lie buried. The town also played an important role in a major challenge to Tudor rule in the 16th century. In 1536, a large procession of northerners, made up of peasants, gentry and Catholic aristocracy, made their way through Yorkshire on the Pilgrimage of Grace. It was led by Robert Aske and was principally a call to Henry VIII and Thomas Cromwell to halt the dissolution of the monasteries and the break with Rome, though the pilgrims had economic grievances as well.

Negotiations between the pilgrims and Henry's representatives were held just outside Doncaster at Cantley Common. Assurances were given to the pilgrims and they dispersed. But the king betrayed them, and Aske and the other

leaders were tried for treason and put to death in the most barbarous fashion.

In the period that concerns us, there was a further fall from grace in Doncaster: its most venerable coaching inn. In *The Old Coaching Days in Yorkshire* (1988), Tom Bradley writes: 'One of the oldest inns on the road was the Old Angel at Doncaster, which was connected with coaching inns from its introduction to its fall, and when stage coaching fell this celebrated old posting house fell with it. Royalty on several occasions honoured it with their presence. In 1603 James I stayed within its walls, while in 1778 His Royal Highness the Duke of York remained at least one night, and a week later the Prince of Wales was an occupant of the state rooms; both rested there on their return journeys in the same month; and the Duke of York again slept here in 1759, whilst noblemen and gentlemen innumerable availed themselves of its excellent accommodation.'

Bradley says that mail coaches used both the Angel and the Red Lion. This was also a major posting house and then coaching inn, where the mayor and his aldermen regularly caroused to such an extent that the mayor was the source of a piece of local doggerel:

The Doncaster mayor sits in his chair,
His mills they merrily go,
His nose doth shine with drinking wine,
And the gout is in his great toe.

Doncaster was a hive of activity. Bradley names some of the famous coaches active in the town: the Highflyer, the Wellington, the Express and the Leeds Union. 'These were all four-horse coaches, leaving Doncaster daily for London,' he records. In total, 14 four-horse coaches were on the road through the town, along with 40 other coaches and between 15 and 20 heavy luggage wagons while a large number of post-chaises and private carriages also hammered through Doncaster.

㉕ Red Lion

37 Market Place, Doncaster, DN1 1NH
01302 732120 www.jdwetherspoon.com

If you manage to cross the snarl of the road between the shopping centre and the old town unscathed, a ginnel leads you into the comparative quiet of the market place. Doncaster is officially called a market town and with good reason. It was given a royal charter in the 12th century to hold a market and it survives to this day. At the far end of the square is the 18th-century Red Lion. The inn is full of pomp and swagger as befits the place where a group of powerful local horse breeders met to organise the first St Leger race on Cantley Common in 1776. As a result, the Red Lion and other inns in the town attracted racegoers from far and wide.

The Red Lion is a shrine to the St Leger, England's oldest horse race. Display boards in the inn list all the winners and their jockeys since the end of World War Two, with Lester Piggott featuring prominently. There are many photos on the walls of both horse racing and the local airport, now named, rather incongruously, after Robin Hood, who was based in the Midlands. There's also memorabilia of WO Bentley, founder of Bentley Motors and – a neat touch, as you clamber upstairs to the toilets – a portrait of Thomas Crapper, who invented the ballcock system. A grateful nation marked his notable improvement to civilised life by turning his name into a vulgar synonym for the lavatory. The Red Lion is now part of the Wetherspoon chain and it's been thoughtfully restored. There are settles, posts, enclosed beams and a large rear garden. Food comes from the standard Wetherspoon menu along with a good range of beers from local breweries, including Daleside and Elland. Accommodation is provided in 15 rooms.

Ferrybridge, West Yorkshire
(181 miles from London, 242 miles to Edinburgh)

Ferrybridge, where the River Aire meets the Aire and Calder canal, is yet a further fall from grace. Today it means the power stations alongside the A1(M) that dominate the horizon for miles around. The stations have been decommissioned and perhaps these blots on the landscape will eventually disappear. It's difficult to imagine that Ferrybridge was once a hive of coach travel when the Great North Road crossed the bridge that gives the village its name. Several substantial coaching inns were grouped around the market place. The Greyhound was a popular stopping point and Charles Dickens was a regular visitor: he wrote parts of *Nicholas Nickleby* there. Another illustrious literary figure connected with

Ferrybridge was Sir Walter Scott. He held regular meetings in the Swan with his literary agent. Scott hated London, his agent disliked Edinburgh so they compromised by discussing Scott's work in the Swan.

The Angel in Ferrybridge was considered to be one of the finest inns on the road, rivalling the George in Stamford in its grandeur and handling 50 pairs of horses a day. But all these inns have disappeared leaving just the Golden Lion that sits beneath the roar of the motorway above. It's a large but spartan pub today and its only beer offering is John Smith's keg ale. I continued on my way knowing I would have better fortune in York.

York
(204 miles from London, 219 miles to Edinburgh)

The county capital can be reached along the A19 via Selby or, from the A1(M), the A64 takes you through the famous brewing town of Tadcaster. 'Taddy' is home to two breweries named Smith – John and Samuel – while a third is a former Bass plant now owned by Molson Coors whose main occupation is making

Carling lager. John and Samuel Smith were members of the same family. They had a serious falling out in the 19th century that led to John marching up the hill and opening his own brewery. Today John Smith's is part of the Heineken UK group while Sam Smith's remains firmly in family hands and is famously traditional, still delivering beer to local pubs by horse-drawn drays.

York is almost beyond words, so rich in history, largely unspoilt, with magnificent buildings dating back over many centuries. The Minster, one of the finest cathedrals in the country, founded in the 11th century, towers majestically over the city while in the cobbled Shambles district, half-timbered medieval buildings lean precariously forward, with their jettied upper storeys forming canopies over the narrow passages below. York has retained its castle and ramparts, with stone gateways marking the early entrances to the city. Micklegate Bar, the most important of these medieval gateways, was the focus of many grand events, though it has a grisly past too: the heads of executed prisoners were displayed above the archway.

York was founded by the Romans in 71AD as Eboracum. This became Jorvik under the Danes and had turned into York by the 13th century. The city's early wealth was based on wool and cloth. It became an important centre for the railways in the 19th century as both a major station and a builder of locomotives, and was also home to two famous chocolate manufacturers, Rowntree and Fry. The city has known turbulence, with skirmishes involving invaders from Northumbria and Scotland. It was besieged by Cromwell's army during the Civil War, with the parliamentary forces going on to defeat the Royalists at Marston Moor. Guy Fawkes, who attempted to blow up parliament, was born in York while Dick Turpin was finally caught and executed in the city. And in spite of the dominant role of the railway in York, the city has held on to some of its celebrated coaching inns.

26 Blue Boar

5 Castlegate, York, YO1 9RN   01904 593209

The Blue Boar's greatest claim to fame is that the body of Dick Turpin was brought to the inn following his execution in 1739. It's alleged (incorrectly) that he was buried here and, in an especially haunted city, there are sightings of his

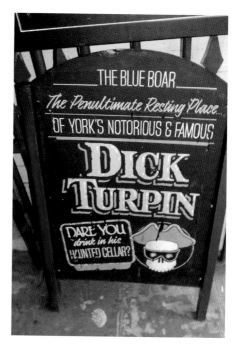

ghost on the spot. The inn has had something of a chequered history. It dates from the early 18th century and has been known as first the Blue Boar, then Robin Hood and finally the Little John. It closed in 2011 but following a vigorous campaign by locals it reopened two years later, with its original name restored. It may have been coincidental but the timing was perfect, as Richard III, son of York, who had been given some late recognition and buried in style in Leicester in 2015, spent his last night before the Battle of Bosworth in the Blue Boar Inn in that city.

The restored Blue Boar in York has a courtyard that once served to welcome coaches. Inside, the inn has wooden floors, booths and plenty of fascinating breweriana. Spiral stairs lead down to a basement where live music and other events are held. Beers comes from good Yorkshire stock – Timothy Taylor and Theakston's – and the food is simple pub grub, with a range of burgers plus scampi and chilli. The inn is handy for the Castle Museum.

㉗ Golden Fleece

16 Pavement, York, YO1 9UP 01904 625171
www.thegoldenfleeceyork.co.uk

If you are interested in ghost hunting, this is the inn for you. It's the most haunted pub in York and possibly the whole country. It's appeared many times

on television and has been visited by the *Most Haunted* team. The inn dates from 1503 and was originally built on stilts without foundations. It was named in honour of the Merchant Adventurers' Guild which had a mansion nearby and whose members drank in the inn. The guild traded in fleeces and their symbol of a golden sheep hangs today as part of the inn sign. It was clearly once a much bigger building but the half-timbered section to the side is now a shop.

Entering the Grade I-listed inn is like taking a step back in time. There are wood panels, beams, old settles, gas lamps and a plethora of prints of old York. An image of Richard III is labelled 'the Yorkist King', a rebuke to Leicester, which claimed his body and buried him there. A panel depicts the 'Life and Crimes of Dick Turpin' – every inn seems to claim him!

The ghosts include One-Eyed Jack who is dressed in 16th or 17th century clothes and armed with a pistol, and a young boy who was trampled to death by horses outside in the 19th century. In 1945 a Canadian airman called Geoff Monroe fell to his death from his bedroom. Guests who stay in his room report being woken in the night by the touch of icy fingers and then seeing a figure dressed in air force uniform. The inn has four rooms for guests – stay if you dare. And best avoid the cellars, where Roman soldiers have been seen.

As well as the comfortable front bar, there's a dining room and a beer garden.

Beers include Black Sheep, Copper Dragon and Timothy Taylor. An extensive menu includes hot and cold sandwiches, soup, jacket potatoes, fishcakes, goat's cheese salad, ploughman's, chicken curry, steak and Stilton pie, and giant Yorkshire puddings with a choice of fillings. The inn is across the road from the Shambles and is also close to the Jorvik Centre.

28 Old White Swan

80 Goodramgate, York, YO1 7LF 01904 540911
www.nicholsonspubs.co.uk

This is a vast inn and it can't be hurried. Sit in its many bars and rooms and soak up a history that dates from the 16th century, while some buildings at the back of the courtyard are even older. The yard itself is where coaches arrived and unloaded and it has a 'mounting stone', a step that enabled passengers to clamber into the coaches.

The inn is part of Nicholson's chain of carefully preserved historic inns and pubs, and the group is to be congratulated on its work in preserving this remarkable building. The Old White Swan, known locally as the 'Mucky Duck', has clearly grown organically over the centuries and is made up of nine structures. They include the beamed Stagecoach Bar and the timber framed Tudor Room, with a large brick hearth and a gallery. Dining takes place in some splendour in the Georgian Room: two Georgian wings were added in 1775 when Goodramgate was widened.

Olde White Swan,
York

Inevitably, the inn is haunted. Spectral figures have been seen sitting round the fire and furniture is sometimes thrown around or rearranged overnight. It's thought that persecuted Catholics in Tudor times hid in the inn before escaping to France. Its main claim to fame dates from 1781 when the world's tallest man, Patrick Cotter O'Brien, was exhibited there. O'Brien was eight feet tall and the landlord charged spectators one shilling – a tidy sum – to see him. O'Brien toured the world and became rich, though he died young in his forties.

The food at the inn is of a high standard and includes beef and ale pie, sea bass, macaroni cheese, Old Spot sausages, and brown rice, quinoa and lemon salad. Eight handpumps dispense a good choice of beer, including Nicholson's house beer, Pale Ale, brewed by St Austell Brewery, and – a rarity – John Smith's Bitter in cask form. The Old White Swan is a popular venue for live jazz.

The delightful interior and, opposite, the courtyard of Ye Olde Starre, York

㉙ Olde Starre

40 Stonegate, York, YO1 8AS 01904 623063
www.taylor-walker.co.uk

The quaint spelling suggests this is a plasterboard recreation from Disneyland. But it's genuine and is possibly York's oldest licensed inn, dating from 1664 as the gallows sign helpfully explains. The sign was erected in 1733 in order to attract customers who might otherwise have missed the narrow entrance. What is called a snickelway leads to a courtyard and gardens with superb views of the Minster: the courtyard has a well that was once the only source of fresh water in the area.

This odd, sideways entrance doesn't prepare you for the delights inside: massive beamed ceilings, latticed and leaded windows, settles, tables fashioned from old wooden beer casks, hatchways, scrubbed wooden floors, coal fires, nooks and crannies, and a bar topped by more leaded lights and a frieze of hops.

The year 1664 was not the best one to open an inn as it coincided with the siege of York by Cromwell's forces during the Civil War. The landlord was a staunch royalist and it's believed the name old star was a subtle way of indicating his support for the king. The parliamentary troops got their own back by using the

cellars as a hospital and mortuary: some of the ghosts – of course the inn is haunted – are seen in the cellars. Another ghost is a Royalist officer dressed in a beaver hat, doublet and breeches.

The inn is at the heart of York's most famous area, the Shambles. The name is ancient and doesn't mean 'a complete mess' as in its modern use but a slaughterhouse. The full and original name is the Great Flesh Shambles and comes from an Anglo-Saxon term meaning the shelves where butchers displayed their meat. As late as 1872 there were 25 butchers in the area but they have all gone, great relief for vegetarians approaching the Olde Starre. The inn is Grade II listed and offers an excellent choice of cask beers, including several from local craft breweries and Taylor Walker's own house beer. A large menu includes fish and chips, burgers, jacket potatoes, sausage and mash, steaks, macaroni cheese and grilled halloumi salad.

On the area

York Minster (01904 557200; www.yorkminster.org)
Jorvik Viking Centre (19 Coppergate, York, YO1 9WT; 01904 615505; www.jorvik-viking-centre.org.uk)
York Castle Museum (Eye of York, York, YO1 9RY; 01904 687687; www.yorkcastlemuseum.org.uk) – Popular history museum that includes the prison cells that once held Dick Turpin.
National Railway Museum (Leeman Road, York, YO26 4XJ; 0844 815 3139; www.nrm.org.uk)
York Brewery (12 Toft Green, York, YO1 6JT; 01904 621162; www.york-brewery.co.uk) – Tours conducted most days and there's a taproom bar on site.
York Tap (York Station, Station Road, York, YO24 1AB; 01904 659009; www.yorktap.com) – Brilliant conversion of the former station tea rooms, with Art Deco ceiling domes and stained glass windows, and a bar serving 18 beers including many from Yorkshire breweries.

Wetherby, West Yorkshire

(215 miles from London, 208 miles to Edinburgh)

Wetherby is a short drive from York but we pass into West Yorkshire: the old market town comes under the jurisdiction of Leeds. It's an important town as it marks the halfway point between London and Edinburgh on the Great North Road, though it's now bypassed by the modern A1(M): in the 18th and 19th century it was an important coaching stage. Wetherby stands on the River Wharfe and it has a fine bridge over the river. The town saw a great deal of activity when Yorkshire was attacked by marauding Scots in the 14th century and at one stage parts of it were burnt to the ground. Cromwell's troops were billeted there during the Civil War before marching on to Marston Moor. During World War Two, the American screen star Clark Gable was stationed at Marston Moor as a member of the US Air Force. When Hitler heard this, he offered an award for anyone who captured the actor. I would like to think Gable responded with his famous last line in *Gone with the Wind*: 'Frankly, my dear, I couldn't give a damn.' Top of the list of famous people born in Wetherby is the revered beer writer Michael Jackson, who died in 2007.

㉚ Swan & Talbot

34 North Street, Wetherby, LS22 6NN
01937 582040 www.swanandtalbot.com

This welcoming inn is more than 400 years old and has a brightly painted, attractive black and white facade and a pleasant rear entrance and beer garden if you ignore the gigantic grocery store

Swan & Talbot

Swan & Talbot

and car park behind. It's claimed the inn's name is unique. It was first called the Swan & Dog, which was the crest of the noble Swann family who lived at Askham Manor. The dog in question was a Talbot, a now extinct breed of hunting dog, and the name was eventually changed to mark the canine's heritage.

During World War Two, troops were garrisoned at the inn. There are photos on the walls of this period, including planes at Marston Moor's Tockwith airfield, plus many other fascinating images of the town and its history. The inn is dominated by a large horseshoe bar that serves what were clearly once two separate bars that have been knocked through into one. There's a vast brick inglenook with a roaring fire on cold days – it was snowing on my visit – and low beams, settles and wood-panelling. There's a large restaurant area that enjoys a good reputation for food:

menus include soup, bruschetta, goat's cheese fritters, sea bass, steaks, burgers, fish and chips, and gnocchi. Beers at the bar feature such local breweries as Rudgate, Black Sheep, Leeds and Timothy Taylor. The inn has four guest rooms.

Boroughbridge, North Yorkshire
(226 miles from London, 197 miles to Edinburgh)

Boroughbridge takes us back into North Yorkshire where the small market town is yet another important old coaching stage, with the A1 crossing the River Ure. The town was destroyed by the Scots in 1318 as they celebrated seizing Berwick-upon-Tweed and then marched further south. But it rose again and by the 18th century the bustling town was a hive of coaching activity as this advertisement in the *Edinburgh Courant* of 1754 shows:

'The Edinburgh Stage-Coach, for the better accommodation of passengers, will be altered to a New Genteel Two-end Glass Coach Machine being on steel springs, exceeding light and easy, to go in ten days in Summer and twelve in Winter, to set out the first Tuesday in March, and continue it, from Hosea Eastgate's the Coach & Horses, in Dean-Street, Soho, London, and from John Somerville's, in the Canongate, Edinburgh, every other Tuesday, and meet at Burrow-Bridge on Saturday

night, and set out from thence on Monday morning, and get to London and Edinburgh on Friday. In Winter to set out from London and Edinburgh every other (alternate) Monday morning, and get to Burrow-Bridge on Saturday night, and set out from thence on Monday morning, and get to London and Edinburgh on Saturday night. Passengers to pay as usual. Performed, if God permits, by your dutiful servant HOSEA EASTGATE.'

'Passengers to pay as usual' suggests there was no increase in fares to pay for the investment in the new coaches: modern train companies please note. The advertisement shows the importance of the Coach & Horses in London's Soho, though it's not clear whether or not coaches started from there or travellers were ferried from the pub to the actual start of the Great North Road. Inns in Boroughbridge made a good living from the coach trade and two contrasting ones have survived.

The Crown Hotel stabling yard in 1900. The round building was the saddle room. The stables, on the right, had rooms for the post boys above

③ Crown Hotel

Horsefair, Boroughbridge, YO51 9LB
01423 322328
www.bw-crownboroughbridge.co.uk

The Crown has a swimming pool! It's the only pool I've encountered on my journey and presumably it would not have been available to coach passengers. It's a plush hotel, part of the Best Western group, and also offers a sauna and beauty salon, which were not mentioned by Mr Hosea Eastgate. But it has kept much of its history, with astonishingly heavy ceiling beams and attractive old settles. It dates from

1300, when it was first the Old Manor House and has retained heavy stone walls, oak trusses and mullioned windows from that time. The walls are decorated with a large number of fascinating old paintings of the coaching period that can be viewed in the bar, with Black Sheep and Rudgate on handpump, and in the restaurant. The wide entrance to the car park was once where coaches arrived and deposited passengers: buildings alongside were the stables that could house up to 100 horses.

The Crown has no fewer than 37

The Stables Bar at the Crown Hotel

guest rooms, some with four-poster beds. The food is excellent and ranges from bar snacks to full meals. Dishes include soup, mushrooms and pancetta, poached asparagus, Barnsley lamb chop, fish pie, sea bass and wild mushroom tortellini. Regular visitors can join the Crown Diners Guild with special offers and priority booking. The inn also has a number of rooms set aside for meetings.

㉜ Black Bull

6 St James Square, Boroughbridge, YO51 9AR
01423 322413 www.blackbullboroughbridge.co.uk

I was welcomed and greeted by name by landlord Tony Burgess, who is proud of his regular listing in the *Good Beer Guide* and several awards from CAMRA. The Black Bull is a delight. From the square it looks like a small community pub but if you turn the corner into the side street you find it stretches for some distance, with a large block set aside as a restaurant. The Grade II-listed building dates from 1257 and was clearly a substantial coaching inn in the 18th and 19th centuries. As you enter from the square you find yourself in a warm and comfortable pub with wood panels, a snug and main bar, a vast inglenook, beamed ceilings, settles and several nooks and crannies. Beer is served through a hatch and foaming pints of John Smith's in cask form and Taylor's Boltmaker quench the thirsts of customers.

Narrow stairs take you up to six guest rooms. The inn has a resident ghost that, Tony says, has an annoying habit of fusing the lights, which makes running a busy pub and restaurant a tad difficult. The food offering includes soup, smoked salmon, steaks, Barnsley chop and Mexican spiced vegetables. Don't miss this one!

Thirsk, North Yorkshire
(238 miles from London, 185 miles to Edinburgh)

Thirsk follows Doncaster, Wetherby and York in having a large racecourse: this one goes on interminably as you drive into the town. But it's worth the wait, for the centre of Thirsk is welcoming and attractive with a large, twice-weekly open air market and an impressive clock tower. It's a popular tourist town as it's a good base for the moors and the dales, with the beauty of Bedale close at hand. And Thirsk has two famous sons. James Herriot is the pen-name of a veterinary surgeon, the world-famous writer of *All Creatures Great and Small*, which became a long-running television series. Thomas Lord achieved fame as the builder of Lord's Cricket Ground in London, the international home of the noble game and headquarters of its governing body, the MCC. Avid cricket lover though I am, I always thought Lord was from Norfolk but, while he did indeed grow up there, he was born in Thirsk.

33 Golden Fleece
Market Place, Thirsk, YO7 1LL O1845 523108
www.goldenfleecehotel.com

This impressive dun-coloured building stands proud alongside the market, the entrance to the left indicating where coaches once entered. Next to the entrance, a taller section of the hotel has impressive arched windows. Inside it's a shrine to both horse racing and the coaching period. An enormous coaching clock stands in the main corridor while the Highflyer Restaurant is named after one of the most famous coaches on the Great North Road.

The inn was built by John and William Hall and it developed from a

The Golden Fleece

posting house into an important coaching stop on the section of the Great North Road between Darlington and York. Around 50 to 60 horses were stabled here and a coach left at 5.30 every morning for London – a dauntingly early start. Portraits of the Halls can be seen in the Drawing Room. Pictures and paintings throughout the hotel depict the history of horse racing in Thirsk, a connection stressed by the Paddock Bar.

There are more rooms than you can wave a riding crop at, including a Writing Room – I wonder if Dickens ever made use of it? – and the Richmond Room. It has everything you would expect of a fine old coaching inn, with architecture encompassing both the Tudor and Adam periods. There are open fires, big settles and heavy beams while some of the 27 guest rooms offer four-poster beds. While it's a spacious hotel, it's not in the least stuffy and you are guaranteed a cheerful Yorkshire welcome. The small and intimate bar has Black Sheep and Copper Dragon on tap, but as I had a long drive south, I settled for afternoon tea and scones. The menu is extensive and includes home-made soup, fishcakes, black pudding fritters, cheddar soufflé, steaks, burgers, fish and chips, lamb rogon josh, and wild mushroom stroganoff.

㉞ Three Tuns

54 Market Place, Thirsk, YO7 1LH 01845 524605
www.jdwetherspoon.com

This Grade II-listed building is only yards from the Golden Fleece and stands on the far corner of Market Place. It predates the Golden Fleece as a coaching inn but started life in 1698 as a dower house for the local Bell family. It had become an inn by 1740 and coaches from London, Edinburgh, Newcastle, Leeds and Darlington used it:

mangers, stalls and hay lofts can be seen at the rear.

It's a palatial building with a large entrance that opens on to a hall with a welcoming fireplace to the right and an impressive Queen Anne pillared staircase ahead that leads up to 13 guest rooms. The hall includes a portrait of Thomas Lord. Perhaps I missed it, but surely there should also be a portrait of William Wordsworth, who spent his honeymoon here in 1802.

The enormous oak bar at the Three Tuns

To the left of the hall, steps take you up to an area set aside for dining, but there's plenty more space further into the inn for eating, where steps lead down to a cellar bar. The main bar area is enormous with a heavy oak bar serving a large range of craft beers along with Adnams, Greene King Abbot and Sharp's Doom Bar on handpumps. As the inn is part of the Wetherspoon chain, it offers the ubiquitous menu, which I can now recite from memory. Accommodation is good value for money.

If you have time, pop into a pub with the curious name of Little 3 at 13 Finkle Street, just off Market Place. It dates from 1214 and was originally known as Ye Olde Three Tuns but the name was changed to avoid confusion with the Three Tuns.

In the area

The World of James Herriot (23 Kirkgate, Thirsk, YO7 1PL; 01845 524234; www.worldofjamesherriot. com) – Museum dedicated to the life and books of Herriot in the building that was his home and surgery.

Thirsk Museum (14-16 Kirkgate, YO7 1PQ; 01845 527707; www.thirskmuseum.org) – Local history museum based in Thomas Lord's former family home.

Thirsk Racecourse (Station Road, Thirsk, YO7 1QL; 01845 522276; www.thirskracecourse.net) – Racing fixtures are held from April to September; other events take place throughout the year.

Northallerton, North Yorkshire
(245 miles from London, 178 miles to Edinburgh)

Northallerton is a fitting place for our final stop in Yorkshire. This ancient market town, which developed from a Roman military camp, is now home to North Yorkshire county council and has for centuries played a leading role in the commerce and politics of the region. Its position on the main road between London and Edinburgh attracted trade when large reserves of phosphorous were discovered and inns sprang up to meet the needs of those dealing in fertiliser and animal feed. A large cattle market attracted drovers who also required accommodation in the town's many inns. The inns were based along the town's impressively long main street and their importance grew further in the age of coach travel.

Northallerton is best known for the Battle of the Standard in 1138, the bloody confrontation between the Scottish army of King David I and the English who rallied around religious banners and standards. The Scots were defeated at terrible cost, with some 12,000 killed.

35 Golden Lion

114 High Street, Northallerton, DL7 8PP
01609 777411 www.golden-lion-hotel.co.uk

The inn dominates the High Street, with its impressive Georgian facade, bowed windows and an entrance with a pillared portico jutting over the pavement. To the right of the main entrance the Coachman's Tap Bar is where coaches entered to drop weary passengers and to change equally weary horses. The hotel

Golden Lion

The lounge at the Golden Lion

is spacious, with wood panelling throughout and a mighty oak bar in the back room used by drinkers. The inn may have 25 guest rooms and elegant restaurants but it does not disguise its history as an inn where much ale was supped by locals and parched travellers. Along with the ubiquitous Greene King IPA, there's a good clutch of Yorkshire brews, including Theakston's Best, Copper Dragon Golden Pippin and Silver Myst, and another welcome sighting of John Smith's Bitter in cask form.

The menus offer, among many dishes, soup, fishcakes, deep fried Brie, chicken and asparagus terrine, salmon fillet, steaks, penne pasta and chargrilled vegetables, and several other vegetarian options. Afternoon tea is also available but first-time visitors might care to sample a branch over the road of a great Yorkshire institution: Betty's Tea Rooms.

③⑥ Black Bull

101 High Street, Northallerton, DL7 8PP
01609 771960 www.blackbullnorthallerton.co.uk

The Black Bull is a modest building when compared to the Golden Lion but it's just as deserved of attention as a genuine coaching inn, as its large arched entrance to the side proves. The cream and green exterior, with bowed windows, welcomes you in to a large L-shaped bar and lounge, with a beamed ceiling, open fires, wood and tiled floor and a heavy oak bar with timber uprights. Handpumped beers include Hobgoblin and Taylor's Landlord. Food

starts with the Breakfast Club for early risers while dishes during the day include chicken Parmesan, scampi and chips, fish and chips and sandwiches – the prawn sandwiches are highly praised. The inn has seven guest rooms.

A visit to the Tickle Toby Inn, 180 High Street, is also recommended. It's named after a notorious 18th-century pickpocket and highwayman and stands in sharp contrast to the opulent Golden Lion opposite.

Road builders

The Turnpike Acts of the 17th and 18th centuries levied tolls along the Great North Road and other highways. The money raised enabled roads to be improved and dramatically increased the comfort of passengers. The first tollgates were erected in the late 17th century on a stretch of the Great North Road between Hertfordshire and Huntingdonshire. Over the following 150 years, some 23,000 miles of roads were covered by 1,000 Turnpike Trusts but it was not until the second half of the 18th century that significant improvements in road making developed.

The first important road builder was the remarkable John Metcalf from Knaresborough in Yorkshire – remarkable because he went blind at the age of six. He nevertheless travelled widely and was contracted to build his first road in 1756. He surveyed and built 150 miles of road in the north of England and died in 1810, aged 93.

Thomas Telford was best known for building bridges but he took great interest in roads. He was born in Scotland in 1757, the son of a shepherd. He went to Edinburgh and worked in the building trade and his experience as a stonemason and structural engineer enabled him to improve the road from London to Holyhead, passing through Bedfordshire. His deep cut in the chalk north of Dunstable was a major engineering feat.

The best-known road builder was another Scot, John McAdam, whose name has gone down in history as the inventor of macadamising. He was born in Ayr in 1756, worked and made a fortune in the United States, and used his own capital to develop his road building system when he returned to Britain.

Macadamising consists of a base of large broken stones on which are laid successive layers of smaller stones. The top dressing formed a compact, smooth, watertight surface. His principle was that if the foundations of the road were kept dry and drained the road would support any weight of traffic.

TOLLS PAID AT BIGGLESWADE GATE.

Stage Coach, Chariot, Post Chaise, or other Carriage of pleasure.	Waggon Wain Cart, &c. 6-inch or upwards.	Waggon, Wain Cart, &c., 4½ inch, and less than 6 inch.	Waggon, Wain Cart, &c less than 4½ inches.	Horse, or Mule, not drawing.	Ass, not drawing.	Score. Oxen, Cows, Calves.	Score. Hogs, Swine Goats, Sheep Lambs, or Geese.	£.	s.	d.
4½d.	2d.	2¼d.	3d.	1d.	½d.	1s. 3d.	5d.			
Horses.	Horses.	Horses.	Horses.							
				1 1 1			1″ 8			
	1	2	2 / 4				1″ 8	0	0	7
			4					0	0	4
			13					0	3	3
		2						0	0	5
	1							0	0	2
13								0	4	10½
								0	9	7½

RECEIVED on *Thursday* the *13*th day of *July* 1854

By *William Cransfield*

5

Darlington to Edinburgh

Edinburgh

46 White Hart
45 Beehive
44 Tolbooth Tavern

Berwick-upon-Tweed

43 Brown Bear

Brown Bear,
Berwick-upon-Tweed

Beehive, Edinburgh

Alnwick

42 Queens Head
41 White Swan

Morpeth

A1

Newcastle

40 County
39 Old George

Old George, Newcastle

Durham
(Shincliffe)

38 Seven Stars

Darlington
(Piercebridge)

37 George

A1 (M)

A1

Northallerton

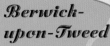

*W*e are now on the second leg of the mighty road, the historic extension that takes us from Yorkshire, England's biggest region, through north-east England and on to Edinburgh. This is border territory, much fought over from the time of the Romans who built Hadrian's Wall to keep the Scots at bay. The road enables us to visit Newcastle, the great power house of the north-east, and on to the disputed border town of Berwick-upon-Tweed before the final sweep of the road to the Scottish capital.

Piercebridge, Darlington
(269 miles from London, 154 miles to Edinburgh)

Piercebridge is officially under the aegis of Darlington but is in a delightful rural spot far removed from the bustle of the major town in County Durham. Darlington became an important industrial centre in the 19th century, building armaments and also bridges that were exported far and wide. It's best known as the town that effectively signalled the end of coach travel when the first passenger train, from Stockton to Darlington, transformed the way in which people moved around the country.

To reach Piercebridge we leave the roar of the A1(M) and are suddenly on an undulating road, the A67, that quickly reaches a village rich in history. A Roman fort was built here between AD 260 and 270. The Romans also threw a bridge across the River Tees in order to continue their journey to the Scottish border along a road known as Dere Street. Parts of the fort are now buried under the village green but the buildings still above ground are open to the public while the stones that formed the Roman bridge lie east of the village at Cliffe.

🐧 George
Piercebridge, Darlington, DL2 3SW 01325 374576
www.thegeorgehotelpiercebridge.com

The address is brief because the inn stands proud and dominant on the main road, a long straddle of barley white buildings with the image of the monarch displayed on the inn sign and above the name on the wall. The 17th-century interior is superb, with oak panels, low beamed ceilings, vast fireplaces, an

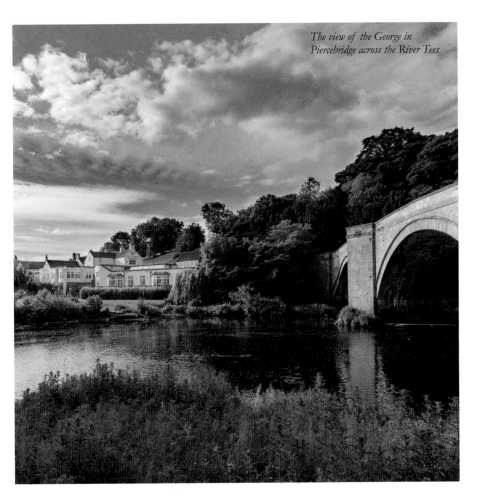

The view of the George in Piercebridge across the River Tees

inglenook and old photos of the area. It's a popular place for meetings, conferences and weddings and has no fewer than 32 guest rooms plus a ballroom. Cabinets display Roman coins and pottery found in the area but the George has a more modern claim to fame: its grandfather clock that's enshrined in a popular song.

In 1875 an American song writer called Henry Clay Work stayed at the George and was intrigued by the story attached to the clock. It had lost time following the death of one of the two Jenkins brothers who owned the George at the time. Eventually the clock stopped completely and Clay Work penned the song *My Grandfather's Clock* that

The bar at the George with a heavy oak counter

includes the line: 'It stopped short never to go again when the old man died'. It's been recorded by a number of singers, including Johnny Cash.

The Snug Bar, with some Art Nouveau flourishes, has a house beer, George Bitter, brewed by Mithril in Aldbrough St John. Food there includes home-made pie and chips, beef lasagne, cod and chips, burgers, Caesar salad, gammon steak, pasta carbonara and vegetable cannelloni. There's a more extensive menu in the Riverside Restaurant overlooking the River Tees.

The famous grandfather clock at the George

𝒪n the area

Piercebridge Roman Fort – Open to the public and admission is free. **Head of Steam railway museum** (Station Road, Darlington, DL3 6ST; 01325 405060; www.darlington.gov.uk) - Home of Stephenson's *Locomotion*, the first steam locomotive to carry passengers on a public railway.

Shincliffe, County Durham

(289 miles from London, 134 miles to Edinburgh)

Shincliffe, a suburb of Durham City and a mile from the city centre, is another village with an important bridge. This impressive structure is medieval and crosses the River Wear but it's thought there may have been a Roman bridge there, too. It's a delightful village and, intriguingly, it was the site of Durham's first railway station in 1834: you can't get away from the nemesis of the coach in these parts!

38 Seven Stars

High Street North, Shincliffe, Co Durham, DN1 2NU 0191 384 8454
www.sevenstarsinn.co.uk

The Seven Stars Inn dates from 1724 and stands at the head of the arrow-straight road through the village. In contrast to the George in Piercebridge, this looks a modest building from the outside but – Tardis-like – it's large and rambling once you step inside. To the right is a charming bar with a welcoming fire, settles, a mass of old photos and prints of the area on the walls, and copper kettles hanging from the ceiling beams. The village is reputed to be the most prosperous area of Durham and this is emphasised by the fact that three large beamed rooms in the inn are set aside for dining and they were all packed to the gunwales when I dropped in. There's also a grandfather clock but this one hasn't stopped.

Beer is not forgotten. The local Durham Brewery's Magus was in pride of place on the bar along with Black Sheep Best and Taylor Landlord when I visited but the choice changes regularly. If you like distilled spirits, Durham Gin and Vodka are also available. Food in the bar includes soup, mushroom risotto and stuffed chicken breast with more extensive menus in the restaurants. There are eight guest rooms and well-behaved dogs are welcome in the bar.

In the area

Durham Cathedral
(0191 386 4266; www.durhamcathedral.co.uk)
Durham Castle (0191 334 2932; www.dur.ac.uk/durham.castle)
A superb choice of pubs in Durham – consult the *Good Beer Guide*. The Old Elm Tree, 12 Crossgate, dates from 1600.

Newcastle upon Tyne
(308 miles from London, 115 miles to Edinburgh)

After the rural tranquillity of Piercebridge and Shincliffe, the A1(M) heads for the metropolitan bustle of Newcastle upon Tyne where famously you didn't need to take coal as so much black gold was mined in the area. The city, one of the most populous in the UK, was also once home to one of the world's biggest shipbuilding and repair centres. But the decline of heavy industry has transformed the area into a thriving modern city based on information technology with a highly regarded university. The city is also a major tourist attraction. Newcastle's past and present is encapsulated in the *Angel of the North*, Antony Gormley's towering sculpture alongside the A1(M) and also visible from the East Coast train line. Standing at 66 feet (20 metres) tall and with wings 177 feet (54 metres) across, it celebrates coal mining and shipbuilding as well as the region's new forms of wealth creation.

Newcastle was founded by the Romans as Pons Aelius and acquired its modern name as a result of a castle built in 1080 by Robert Curthose, the eldest son of William the Conqueror. The city played a strategic role in the long struggle between the English and the Scots. The early wealth of the city was based on the wool trade before mining took over and later shipbuilding came to the fore in the 19th century.

Newcastle's pomp and grandeur is summed up by its position alongside the River Tyne, its great trading artery. A series of soaring bridges straddle the river, linking the city with Gateshead. One of the most iconic buildings, the former Rank Hovis Baltic flour mill, has been transformed into the Baltic Centre for Contemporary Art beside the Millennium Bridge. As well as exhibitions and concerts, visitors can see magnificent views of the region from the top of the building.

The local people are famously known as Geordies, a much disputed name. Some say it's a term of abuse from

The beamed bar of the Old George, Newcastle's last remaining coaching inn

the Scots used during the Jacobite rebellion in 1745 when staunch supporters of George II defended the city. A more modern version says it's derived from the great engineer George 'Geordie' Stephenson who not only built steam locomotives in the 19th century but also designed a safety lamp for coal miners known as a 'Geordie lamp'. The distinctive Geordie dialect is descended from the Early English language of the Anglo-Saxon settlers in the area.

39 Old George

Old George Yard, Newcastle upon Tyne, NE1 1EZ
0191 260 3035 www.oldgeorgeinnnewcastle.co.uk

The Old George, built in 1582, is Newcastle's only remaining coaching inn in an area of local history that has hung on by its finger tips and survived the ravages of inner-city renewal. The inn is found down a cobbled courtyard in Bigg Market, once one of many open-air markets along the Great North Road. Bigg is the name for an early type

On the area

Angel of the North (Durham Road, Gateshead, NE9 7TY) – Antony Gormley's magnificent steel sculpture. The site is accessible on foot and parking is available nearby.

Baltic Centre for Contemporary Art (South Shore Road, Gateshead, NE8 3BA; 0191 478 1810; www.balticmill.com)

Great North Museum (Barras Bridge, Newcastle upon Tyne, NE2 4PT; 0191 208 6765; www.greatnorthmuseum.org.uk) – Natural history museum with a varying programme of exhibitions.

Discovery Museum (Blandford Square, Newcastle upon Tyne, NE1 4JA; 0191 232 6789; www.discoverymuseum.org.uk) – Local history museum and home to *Turbinia*, once the fastest steam-powered ship in the world.

Crown Posada (31 Side, Newcastle upon Tyne, NE1 3JE; 0191 232 1269) – vies with the Old George as the city's oldest pub. Architecturally fine interior and on CAMRA's list of pubs with interiors of historic importance.

of barley, sold from stalls, and used for baking bread and making ale when they were domestic pursuits. Bigg Market once had 31 listed buildings, most of them have been thoughtlessly knocked down, but the Old George has survived and has been carefully renovated by its current owners, the Stonegate pub company.

The courtyard is more than an entrance. In good weather, customers can sit there to enjoy a drink and chat while bands and buskers sometimes perform there too. Inside, there's a feeling of great antiquity, with beams, open fires, and stairs and corridors that creak with age. It's said to be haunted and in a very grand manner. Charles I was held in an open prison in the city by the Scots in 1646 and he was allowed to visit the inn on a regular basis. There's a King Charles Room and even the chair where he sat: his ghostly figure has apparently been seen there.

The main bar has a bank of five handpumps in a cabinet dispensing beer and there are more pumps in a smaller side bar. Six beers rotate frequently but you will find one regular to relish: Draught Bass, now a rarity, sidelined by its global owner AB InBev, but a link to the great beers of Burton-on-Trent in Victorian England. Food starts with breakfast, served until 12 noon, and dishes at other times include sandwiches, grills, tapas, pies, salads and burgers.

40 County

High Street, Gosforth, Newcastle upon Tyne,
NE3 1HB 0191 285 6919 www.johnbarras.com

The address is the High Street but this is the Great North Road, heading north through the suburb of Gosforth. The County is a large and imposing street-corner building dating from 1826. Local mobsters, the Bulman family, built it but it became respectable when James Stark bought it in 1866. Stark sold it on for £6,000 to James Deuchar in 1881.

Deuchar brewed and ran pubs in Newcastle and Sunderland before buying a brewery in Montrose in Scotland. He was eventually taken over by Scottish & Newcastle Breweries that also acquired another Deuchar, Robert of that ilk, in Leith, who had become a major producer of India Pale Ale. Deuchar's IPA lives on today, produced by the Caledonian Brewery.

The County belongs to the John Barras pub group, once part of Scottish &

Newcastle. It became the Spirit Group, bought by Greene King: the Suffolk brewer has a sizeable stake in Scotland and the north-east through its ownership of the Belhaven brewery in Dunbar. The County's main L-shaped room is large with high ceilings and some attractive stained glass windows overlooking the high street. There's a large oak bar and plenty of seating. A second, smaller room can be hired for meetings and functions. A sizeable garden by the side entrance has benches, tables and flowering tubs. The beers just have to include Deuchar's IPA, along with the ubiquitous Greene King IPA, plus ale from the local Wylam Brewery and six more rotating beers. Food includes steaks, burgers, chick pea curry, nachos and filled jacket potatoes.

Morpeth, Northumberland
(321 miles from London, 102 miles to Edinburgh)

The A1(M) takes us on into Northumberland, the final English county before Scotland. It's the least populated county but has the largest number of castles, the result of centuries of battles between the English and the Scots. The Percy family, the earls of Northumberland, wielded great power for centuries and one of them, Sir Henry – known as Harry Hotspur – was immortalised by Shakespeare and bequeathed his name to a London football club: the family owned land in North London, including Northumberland Park in Tottenham. The county is also the cradle of Christianity: Saint Adrian built a priory on Holy Island or Lindisfarne in the sixth century and monks used the island as a base for spreading the gospels throughout the north-east. It's a region of sweeping moorlands and unspoilt beaches with small towns of historic importance and fine buildings.

Sadly, the fine building I had come to find in Morpeth is closed and derelict. The Queen's Head, which dominates Bridge Street, is a sprawling half-timbered, black and white Tudor inn that shut in 2015. Locals have demonstrated their displeasure outside and have condemned plans by a property developer to turn the site into a 'boutique hotel'. An important part of coaching history is destined to be lost. On a positive note, I would like to thank the kind folk in Specsavers opposite the Queen's Head who restored one lens in my glasses that had popped out in disbelief when I saw the inn shuttered, barred and covered in graffiti and posters.

Alnwick, Northumberland

(339 miles from London, 84 miles to Edinburgh)

To describe Alnwick as breathtaking doesn't begin to do the market town justice. It's steeped in history, with unspoilt medieval buildings and a castle that was (and still is) the ancestral home of the Percy family, the baronial overlords of Northumberland. The castle was built on land donated by William the Conqueror. Alnwick – pronounced 'Annick' – stands on the River Aln, was founded in AD 600 and was much fought over for centuries by the Percys and the marauding Scots. A cross at Broomhouse Hill marks the spot where Malcolm III of Scotland was killed during the First Battle of Alnwick in 1093. The Scots got their own back when they twice burnt most of the town in 1424 and

1448. It recovered and later became an important staging post on the Great North Road.

Market Place marks the centre of the town, entered through the medieval Hotspur Tower that divides Bondgate Without from Bondgate Within. Once through the gate we can visit the two contrasting coaching inns that have survived.

41 White Swan

Bondgate Within, Alnwick, NE66 1TD

01665 602109   www.classiclodges.co.uk

The White Swan is sumptuous. It commands one side of Bondgate Within and while it's 18th century in origin its main claim to fame is that it's a static

The Oympic Suite at the White Swan with fittings from the sister ship to the Titanic

version of the ill-fated RMS *Titanic* that sank in the Atlantic in 1912. The *Titanic* had a sister ship, the RMS *Olympic*, which had an almost identical design. The owner of the White Swan, Algernon Smart, sailed on her frequently. When the ship was broken up Smart acquired many of the fixtures and fittings and installed them at the inn. Today, the centrepiece of the White Swan is the Olympic Suite with panelled walls, mirrors, an ornate ceiling, a marble fireplace and a staircase from the ship. The revolving doors at the entrance to the inn also come from the *Olympic*.

It's not the first time the Grade II-listed White Swan has been given an expensive makeover. In 1852, the Duke of Northumberland employed one of the top architects of the day, Anthony Slavin,

to remodel his castle and Slavin also spent some time upgrading the inn, which was expanded into neighbouring buildings.

As a result, as well as the Olympic Suite, there are more spacious and opulent rooms, tiled and carpeted, with open fires and many paintings of Alnwick and Northumberland. There are 55 guest rooms and two restaurants offering varied menus. The chefs use local ingredients whenever possible and dishes may include vegetable spring roll, mackerel fillet, pork terrine, confit of duck, sea bream, and leek and blue cheese tart. There's a house beer supplied by the Alnwick Brewery: considering the *Titanic* connections, best not to say the beer went down well.

42 Queens Head

25 Market Street, Alnwick, Northumberland, NE66 1SS 01665 604691

The Queens Head is just yards from the White Swan but couldn't be more different. This is a homely, welcoming community pub that claims to be the oldest inn in Alnwick dating from 1777, though some say the 16th century. A queen on the inn sign makes a welcome change from all the Georges we have encountered on this long journey. It stands opposite a large row of buildings known as the Shambles that houses the local information centre and a number of craft shops but, in common with the Shambles in York, it was first used as a slaughterhouse as well as a meeting

place for local societies.

Next to the inn's entrance there's a large archway indicating where coaches once entered. It was occupied by a motorbike on my visit and clearly has adapted to modern modes of transport. Inside, the Queens Head is bright and airy with two bars that have been knocked through into one. It has covered beams, open fires and settles, heavy oak serving counters, and a large number of photos of the area, including Alnwick Castle. The kitchen and dining area at the rear has several oak beer casks.

Alnwick Brewery supplies Amber Ale and there's a second, rotating beer on handpump. Food includes fresh fish from Whitby along with grills, burgers and a weekend carvery. There are three guest rooms. I enjoyed a chat with the locals at the bar: it's that sort of place. There are regular live music events.

In the area

Alnwick Castle (NE66; 01665 511100; www.alnwickcastle. com) – Home to the Percy family for over 700 years, the castle has lavish state rooms and also contains the Fusiliers Museum. The castle has featured in two *Harry Potter* films and in television's *Downton Abbey*. It is open to the public from March to October.

Alnwick Garden (NE66 1YU; 01665 511350; www.alnwickgarden. com) – Redeveloped at the start of the 21st century, this stunning contemporary garden has a giant water cascade and one of the largest treehouses in the world.

Berwick-upon-Tweed, Northumberland

(367 miles from London, 56 miles to Edinburgh)

The last English stretch of the A1 is a reminder of what the old Great North Road was like. It's a straight, narrow, two-lane highway quite different to the newer motorway sections further south. It also runs through some of the most magical areas of north-east England with road signs tempting drivers to stay awhile and visit the beautiful coastal town of Alnmouth, Holy Island reached by a causeway, the Farne Islands with their colonies of grey seals, and the historic castles of Bamburgh and Dunstanburgh. But we cannot linger and must hurry on to Berwick-upon-Tweed, just 2½ miles from the border with Scotland.

Berwick is to England and Scotland what the Strasbourg region is to France and Germany, disputed and long fought-over territory. It began as an Anglo-Saxon settlement and became an important town in the Kingdom of Northumbria. The 'Ber' at the start of the name – in common with Bigg, the Newcastle market – is an old term for a type of barley, with 'wick' meaning settlement: the town was an important source of grain for bread and ale production.

It was annexed by England in the 10th century and changed hands several times, the last in 1482 when it returned once more to England. It was a wealthy town in Tudor times as the English poured money in to build walls and ramparts to stop the Scots seizing the town again. The battles may not over: the current Scottish government has hinted that Berwick should be part of their domain. And the issue is clouded by the fact that both Berwick's football and rugby teams play in Scottish divisions.

The town is famous for its bridges spanning the Tweed. The Old Bridge dates from 1610 and was supplemented in 1821 by the Union, the world's oldest suspension bridge. Then in 1847 the great engineer Robert Stephenson spanned the river with the awesome Royal Border Bridge, a railway viaduct 720 yards (658 metres) long that affords train passengers with an inspiring view of the river below. Not surprisingly, a town that played a key role in the movement of people and goods along the Great North Road had some fine coaching inns.

The 16th-century Kings Head in Church Street is an impressive building with grey stone upper storeys and a brown and white ground floor. It stands on an ancient road that was once called

Soutergate – street of shoemakers. The inn survived an attempt by the mayor of Berwick in the 16th century to close many of the town's inns as a result of riotous behaviour by the locals. Its large side entrance and cobbled courtyard show it was an important coaching inn. The inn has guest rooms and food is served but the pub has no real ales.

🐻 Brown Bear

27 Hide Hill, Berwick-upon-Tweed, Northumberland, TD15 1EQ 01289 298258
www.berwickbrownbear.co.uk

The Brown Bear is Berwick's oldest inn and it takes its name from the town's coat of arms. It was rebuilt in 1898 but its date of origin is not known for the good reason that the inn was run down and neglected for many years and was brought back to life in late 2016 just in time to be included in this book. A landlady had run the Brown Bear for 18 years and wanted to retire. The owner, Britain's biggest pub company Enterprise Inns, put it up for auction and it was bought by a local builder called Frank Flannigan. He was lobbied by locals who appealed to him to keep the building as a pub and he agreed to sell it to Mark Dodds and his partner, his parents and supporters.

By good fortune I arrived in Berwick the morning after the Brown Bear had reopened the night before. It's an impressive building, its modest facade giving no hint of the size of the interior. It has low ceilings, old settles, alcoves and many nooks and crannies. The oak bar runs the length of the front bar and the back has space for live entertainment with the kitchen beyond. Local historian Jim Herbert of Berwick Time Lines has researched the history of the Brown Bear and says architect's plans for the inn in 1806 show buildings at the rear that were almost certainly used for stabling horses. There was also a blacksmith's shop nearby for shoeing horses. There was a much bigger side entrance in the early 19th century to accommodate coaches. The landlord at the time ran a coach service to Kelso.

Mark Dodds plans to provide accommodation when the restoration work on the ground floor is complete. He is an experienced publican and an outspoken critic of the large pub companies that run more than half of Britain's pubs. His battles with the 'pubcos' in London led to him setting up the Fair Pint campaign and he was happy to return to the north-east as his family come from the Newcastle and Morpeth area. He has been given great support from the Hadrian & Border brewery in Newburn close to Newcastle and their Tyneside Blonde, Reiver, Secret Kingdom and Northumberland Gold beers are on the bar along with Alnwick Brewery's Village Lite.

By early 2017, the Brown Bear had started to serve food and it has rapidly built a strong local following for live music events. It has become a hub of the community once again.

Edinburgh
(423 miles from London)

And now the road takes us into Scotland and on the final sweep to its last destination, Edinburgh. Charles Harper, writing in 1901, said, 'The distant view of Edinburgh is magnificent. The peaked and jagged masses of Arthur's Seat and Salisbury Craigs [sic], the monument-cumbered Calton Hill, the Castle Rock – all these combine to make the traveller eager to reach so picturesque a spot.' But distance lends enchantment to the view. Today Edinburgh's Old and New Towns are together inscribed as a UNESCO World Heritage Site but the elegant city we now know had a more squalid past. The Old Town in the 18th century was described as one of the most over-crowded and insanitary areas in Britain. Its nickname of Auld Reekie (old smelly) is disputed. Some say it came from the number of breweries belching smoke and the fumes of malts and hops into the air. Others – who are probably correct – claim it stemmed from the stink of the tenements and the habit of discharging the contents of chamber pots on to the cobbles and heads of unwary passers-by with the cry of 'gardy-loo'. This came from the French *gardez-l'eau* or 'beware the water', one of the least appetising aspects of the Old Alliance between Scotland and France. The better-off departed for the Georgian splendours of the New Town while the Old Town was transformed in the 1860s into the Victorian area known today. 'Urban renewal' and the arrival of the steam train meant that most of Edinburgh's coaching inns were demolished, deemed no longer fit for purpose. If that is disappointing where this book is concerned, travellers in the 18th and 19th centuries would have greeted the disappearance of those hostelries with joy. For Edinburgh's coaching inns were far removed from those in England. As Harper records, 'Instead of putting up at some fine hospitable inn, such as they were used to even in the smaller English towns, they [travellers] were set down at a "stabler's", the premises of one whose first business was to horse the coaches and to let saddle-horses, and who, as in some sort of after-thought, lodged those who were obliged to journey about the country.'

One traveller arriving in Edinburgh in 1774 wrote: 'One can scarcely form in the imagination the distress of a miserable stranger on his first entrance into this city. On my first arrival, my companion and self, after the fatigue of a long day's journey, were landed at one of these stable-keepers in a part of the town which is called the Pleasance; and on entering the house were conducted by a poor girl

The Edinburgh Express, 1837

without shoes or stockings, and with only a single linsey-woolsey petticoat which reached halfway to her ankles, into a room where about twenty Scotch drovers had been regaling themselves with whisky and potatoes. You may guess our amazement when we were informed that this was the best inn in the metropolis, and that we could have no beds unless we had an inclination to sleep together, and in the same room with the company which a stage-coach had that moment discharged.'

Another less than satisfied customer was the much-travelled Dr Samuel Johnson who reached Edinburgh in 1773

and booked into the White Horse in Boyd's Close, described as 'that dirty and dismal inn' kept by James Boyd. The doctor immediately sent a note to James Boswell: 'Saturday night – Mr Johnson sends his compliments to Mr Boswell, being just arrived at Boyd's.' Boswell hurried to the inn to find the doctor in a foul mood. He was not only unimpressed by the dirty facilities but also enraged by a waiter who had sweetened Johnson's lemonade by using his fingers rather than sugar tongs. According to Boswell, Johnson threw the lemonade out of the window [gardy-loo?] and seemed inclined to throw the waiter after it.

In spite of the squalor of the inns, there was good money to be made. Peter Ramsay's was a well-known inn at the foot of St Mary's Wynd, next to Cowgate Port. Ramsay advertised it in 1776 as 'a good house for entertainment, good stables for above one hundred horses, and sheds for about twenty carriages.' It was considered one of the best hostelries in Edinburgh and yet the beds were described as 'dish clouts stretched on grid irons.' Ramsay nevertheless profited well and he retired in 1790 with a fortune of £10,000.

For good or bad, these inns and stablers are long gone and we end our journey with the few historic hostelries that remain, the first of which is in the Canongate, the original departure point in Edinburgh for coaches to London.

The charms of the Canongate were not lost on local writers and poets. Sir Walter Scott, whose life – 1771–1832 – neatly coincides with the heyday of coach travel, wrote: 'Sir Sic itur ad Astria; This is the Path to Heaven. Such is the ancient motto attached to armorial bearings of the Canongate, and which is inscribed with greater or less propriety, upon all public buildings, from the church to the pillory, in the ancient quarter of Edinburgh which bears, or rather once bore, the same relation to the Good Town that Westminster does to London.' That inveterate user of coach travel, Charles Dickens, developed the plots for both *Great Expectations* and

A Christmas Carol while staying in the Canongate: the fact that the Tolbooth is one of Edinburgh's most haunted buildings may have helped with the latter story.

The magnificent grey stone building of the Tolbooth, with its soaring turrets and imposing, intimidating clock overhanging the street, is locked into the turbulent history of Scotland's capital city. It was built in 1591 to collect fees from travellers. At the time Canongate, founded by David I of Scotland, was a separate borough or burgh outside the walls of the city: the first part of the name paid homage to the canons of Holyrood Palace while gate is an ancient word for passageway.

The Tolbooth housed council chambers, a police court and a prison. The front part of the building was transformed into a tavern in 1820 and the familiar curved entrance to the side of the building leading to a wynd or alley was clearly designed to allow coaches to enter.

But all was not sweetness and light at the Tolbooth. The prison conditions were appalling and it was the scene of public executions: large crowds would pack the narrow Canongate to see prisoners hanged or beheaded on gallows erected outside the building. Leaders of the Covenanters, the 17th-century Presbyterian movement ruthlessly hunted down by the Catholic establishment, were among the victims. The Dukes of Montrose and Argyll were beheaded

outside the Tolbooth, their heads placed on spikes as a grisly warning to others.

The English Civil War, despite the name, made an impact in Scotland. Oliver Cromwell stayed twice in the Canongate while his New Model Army fought the supporters of Charles I. In 1654, Cromwell's guards detained Royalists in the Tolbooth prison but the building couldn't hold them and they made their escape in the time-honoured fashion of using strips of blankets to lower themselves from the upper floor. Other prisoners were less fortunate. Many were sentenced to seven years hard labour and were transported to work on sugar plantations in the West Indies. Women were branded on the face while male prisoners each had an ear chopped off.

44 Tolbooth Tavern

167 Canongate, Edinburgh, EH8 8BN
0131 629 4500 www.tolboothedinburgh.co.uk

The Tolbooth Tavern today is a tranquil place. You enter through a surprisingly modest door into a front bar with a carved wooden serving counter, while a flight of stairs takes you to a spacious dining room. The history of the Tolbooth and Canongate is presented on the walls with ancient prints, photos and maps. Beers come from the local Caledonian Brewery and include Deuchars IPA and Flying Scotsman. The extensive menu reflects the history of the building with a degree of humour: Warlock Pie recalls the event in 1591 when a male witch or

warlock was exorcised there. A range of burgers includes The Jailer, Cromwell's Revenge and The Gallows. Traditional haggis is also available and there are many vegetarian and vegan options.

The final two inns stand on the Grassmarket in Edinburgh's Old Town. It's now a large square with hotels, restaurants, pubs and smart houses but for centuries it was a large open-air market and a place of execution. A market was established in the 15th century. Drovers brought sheep and cattle there and it took on the name of Grassmarket from the sight of livestock eating grass in their pens. It developed into Edinburgh's major market place. Daniel Defoe visited the square in the 1720s and described it as 'This street, which is called the Bow, is generally full of wholesale traders, and those very considerable dealers in iron, pitch, tar, oil, hemp, flax, linseed, painter's colours, dyers, drugs and wood, and such like heavy goods, and supplies country shopkeepers, which our wholesale dealers in England do.'

The Grassmarket's macabre side was as a place of execution. In *The Heart of Midlothian*, Sir Walter Scott described in graphic detail the horror of seeing the giant gibbet being erected early in the morning in preparation for hangings during the day. More than 100 Covenanters died on the gallows between 1661 and 1688, a period known as the Killing Time. One inn on the

The spacious bar of the Tolbooth Tavern that specialises in beers from the local Caledonian Brewery

Grassmarket is called the Last Drop: prisoners waiting to be hanged were allowed one final drop of whisky. Even when hanging stopped, the Grassmarket was not immune to death: an inscribed flagstone on the pavement in front of the White Hart shows where a bomb exploded during a Zeppelin raid on Edinburgh in April 1916, killing 11 people.

As the arched entrances around the square show, the Grassmarket in the 18th and 19th centuries became an important staging post for coaches. In the late 18th century the coach to London via Dumfries and Carlisle set out from an inn at Cowgate Head at the eastern end of the market. This is also possibly the route taken by William and Dorothy Wordsworth, who came to Edinburgh in 1803 and took rooms at the White Hart on the Grassmarket. Dorothy described it as 'not noisy and tolerably cheap'.

45 Beehive

18-20 Grassmarket, Edinburgh, EH1 2JU
0131 225 7171 www.taylor-walker.co.uk

There's been an inn on the site since the 15th century though this is a more modern building. There are seats on the pavement for eating and drinking in warm weather with Edinburgh Castle looming overhead. The interior is spacious with both wood and carpeted floors and a wealth of photos and prints of the Grassmarket and Edinburgh on the walls. There are enclosed ceiling beams and standing timbers, details of the history of the inn and an enigmatic sign saying: 'On the 14th April 1841, on this spot, nothing happened'. One portrait of locals shows William Burke, one half of the 19th century body-snatching duo Burke and Hare: see the next entry for more about them.

The main bar is called the Honeypot where customers can dine and choose

from a menu that includes sandwiches, burritos, jacket potatoes, fish and chips, curry, pies and burgers. There are side rooms, nooks and crannies where you can enjoy a quiet drink without eating; beers come from the Greene King range, including its Scottish subsidiary Belhaven of Dunbar, and there is often one guest beer from an independent Scottish brewery. The inn has regular entertainment and is home to the Beehive Comedy club. It's also an important venue for music and comedy during the Edinburgh Fringe.

46 White Hart

34 Grassmarket, Edinburgh, EH1 2JU
0131 226 2806 www.whitehart-edinburgh.co.uk

The White Hart claims to be the city's oldest inn, dating from 1516 and the large arched entrance to the side shows that it was once an important coaching inn. Its name comes from a legend that tells how King David I went hunting in the area in 1128 on the Feast Day of the Holy Rood (rood is Scottish for cross). He saw a giant white stag and gave chase but was thrown from his horse. The enraged animal turned on the king, who prayed for deliverance. A fiery cross appeared between the antlers of the beast, which promptly disappeared. A grateful monarch founded Holyrood Abbey to mark his deliverance but the white hart was not forgotten and became a heraldic symbol. The legend becomes believable with a glass or two of the finest Highland malt.

The heavily beamed interior of the White Hart is engraved with quotations from the poet Robert Burns. He came to the inn in 1791 on his final visit to

Quotations from Robert Burns are etched on the beams of the White Hart

On the area

The People's Story (Canongate Tolbooth, Royal Mile, Edinburgh, EH8 8BN; 0131 529 4057; www.edinburghmuseums.org.uk) – Museum in the same building as the Tolbooth Tavern that tells the story of ordinary Edinburgh people from the late 18th century to the present day.

Arthur's Seat – Remains of an ancient volcano and the highest point in Holyrood Park, Edinburgh. It's worth climbing for the excellent views over the city.

Edinburgh Castle (0131 310 5114; www.edinburghcastle.gov.uk)

Holyrood Palace (Canongate, Royal Mile, Edinburgh, EH8 8DX; 0303 123 7334; www.royalcollection.org.uk) – The Queen's official residence in Scotland, open to the public all year round.

Caledonian Brewery (42 Slateford Road, Edinburgh, EH11 1PH; 0131 337 1288; www.caledonianbeer.com) – Traditional brewery that uses direct-flame copper kettles and produces the award-winning Deuchars IPA. Tours can be arranged.

Edinburgh to see his lover Nancy Macklehose and was inspired to write the poem *Ae Fond Kiss*. Other prominent visitors have included Oliver Cromwell and the Wordsworths. Images of Burke and Hare are also on display. In 1828 they would visit the White Hart and other inns in the area and entice drinkers back to their lodgings where they killed them and handed over the corpses to Dr Knox at Edinburgh Medical School. Not surprisingly, the White Hart is said to be haunted.

The inn has a wonderful historic feel to it with its beams, old settles and green-painted wooden walls. The main building dates from the 18th century but the original cellars are from the 16th. The beers come from Belhaven and include IPA, 80 Shilling and Dark Island. An extensive menu includes haggis in a number of guises. Food and drink can be enjoyed at the front in an enclosed area on the pavement and, in common with the neighbouring Beehive, the White Hart hosts regular live entertainment.

Quotations

Coaching inns and the journeys between them have been discussed often in literature. Here is a selection of quotations on the subject from some famous writers of the past.

The main roads of England are incomparable for excellence, of a beautiful smoothness, very ingeniously laid down, and so well kept that in most weathers you could take your dinner off any part of them without distaste ... No, nowhere in the world is travel so great a pleasure as in that country.

Robert Louis Stevenson, *St Ives*, 1897

A regular character was that old ostler: he was a Yorkshireman by birth but he had seen a great deal of life in the vicinity of London.

George Borrow

Then let's meet here, for here are fresh sheets that smell of lavender: and I am sure we cannot expect better meat or better usage in any place.

Izaak Walton, on staying in an inn in Newark

The great clown Joseph Grimaldi was an early commuter and would travel from his home in the village of Highgate to the London theatres. Just south of Islington on the first stage out of the city the road passes Sadler's Wells theatre and Grimaldi often appeared there. One night in 1807, on his way home, he was stopped by footpads on Highgate Hill, but when he showed them his watch, engraved with his likeness, they recognised him and let him go.

Louise Allen, Jane Austen's London

There is a certain relief in change, even though it be from bad to worse; as I have found in travelling in a stage coach, that it is often a comfort to shift one's position and be bruised in a new place.

Washington Irving

The incognito of an inn is one of its striking privileges.

William Hazlitt

Two inches to the north-west is written a word full of meaning – the most purposeful word that can be written on a map. 'Inn'.

AA Milne

How fine it is to enter some old town, walled and turreted, just at approach of nightfall, or to come to some straggling village, with the lights streaming through the surrounding gloom; and then, after inquiring for the best entertainment that the place affords, to 'take one's ease at one's inn!'

William Hazlitt

When you have lost your inns drown your empty selves, for you will have lost the last of England.

Hillaire Belloc

We dined at an excellent inn at Chapel-house, where he expatiated on the felicity of England in its taverns and inns, and triumphed over the French for not having, in any perfection, the tavern life. 'There is no private house, (said he), in which people can enjoy themselves so well, as at a capital tavern'. He then repeated, with great emotion, Shenstone's lines:

Whoe'er has travell'd life's dull round,
Where'er his stages may have been,
May sigh to think he still has found
The warmest welcome at an inn.

James Boswell

Bibliography

Sources and further reading

James Boswell, *The Life of Samuel Johnson*, 1791

William C Boswell, *Along the Great North Road*, 1939

Tom Bradley, *Old Coaching Days in Yorkshire*, 1988

Charles Dickens, *Nicholas Nickleby*, 1839

Charles Dickens, *A Tale of Two Cities*, 1859

Charles G Harper, *The Great North Road: London to York*, 1901, revised edition 1922

Charles G Harper, *The Great North Road: York to Edinburgh*, 1901, revised edition 1922

Thomas Hughes, *Tom Brown's Schooldays*, 1857

Frank Morley, *The Great North Road*, 1961

JB Priestley, *The Good Companions*, 1929

Films featuring the Great North Road

They Drive by Night, a film featuring the Great North Road, appeared in 1938. It starred Emlyn Williams, Ernest Thesiger and Ronald Shiner, with a small part for William Hartnell, who achieved fame later as the first Dr Who. The film is based on a novel of the same name by James Curtis. The 'film noire' was praised for its authentic portrayal of both criminals and the life of truck drivers. Graham Greene, who was the film critic for The Spectator, wrote: 'They Drive by Night is a murder-story set against an authentic background of dance palaces, public houses, seedy Soho clubs, and the huge wet expanse of the Great North Road, with is bungaloid cafes, the grinding gears, and the monstrous six-wheeled lorries plunging through the rain.'
Greene's film reviews were collected in *Mornings in the Dark*, 1993.

The Leather Boys, 1964, starred Rita Tushingham and featured bikers from the famous Ace Cafe on London's North Circular Road who held an annual race to and from Edinburgh in a day along the Great North Road.

Index of featured pubs

Picture credits

T Allom & T Clark, folio print 102; Artist unknown, old print 10, 87, 113; Matt Brown/flickr 114 (bottom); deargdoom57/flickr 124; John Dockray 130, 131; Mark Dodds 168; Martin Ellis 156; Nick Forshaw 88, 89; Tim Green/flickr 138; Cath Harries 25, 26, 36, 126, 128; T Hosmer Shepherd, from a drawing by 13, 14; James Pollard, print after 15, 171; Travis Hudson, Head of Marketing, Lion, Buckden 66; Steve Parker, Hampton Cheese and Wine Company 79; Roger Protz 17, 19 (top and bottom right), 20, 29, 35, 39, 45, 46, 47, 48, 49 (top and bottom), 53, 54, 61, 63, 64, 67, 69, 71, 72, 73, 74, 80, 93, 96, 98, 99, 100, 103, 105, 107, 114 (top), 119, 123, 129, 144, 154, 160, 165, 167, 173, 175, 176, 177, 179; Stilton Community Association 78; Stockwood Discovery Centre (images courtesy of Luton Culture) 57, 147; Roberto Strauss/flickr 125

The author and publisher would also like to thank all the pubs, inns and hotels that have kindly contributed photographs to this book.

Acknowledgements

Thanks to both Katie Button and Julie Hudson at CAMRA Books for help with compiling lists, sorting out geography, sourcing images, and knocking the manuscript into shape. CAMRA's Pubs Heritage Group and CAMRA branches have been a great help by both recommending pubs and answering queries. The following deserve special mentions: Dave Gamston and Andrew Davison in York, and Martin Ellis and John Holland in Newcastle. Thanks also to Highgate Historical Society, Edinburgh Historical Society, Enfield & Barnet Libraries, and St Neots Local History Society. Special thanks are due to the publicans and hoteliers who were generous with their time and whose passion for their ancient inns fuelled my enthusiasm. I must stress though that the final selection of inns is mine.

Books for beer lovers

CAMRA Books is the publishing arm of the Campaign for Real Ale and the leading publisher of books on beer, pubs, brewing and beer tourism. Some of our key titles include:

Good Beer Guide 2017

Editor: Roger Protz

CAMRA's *Good Beer Guide* is fully revised and updated each year and features pubs across the United Kingdom that serve the best real ale. Now in its 44th edition, this pub guide is completely independent with listings based entirely on nomination and evaluation by CAMRA members. This means you can be sure that every one of the 4,500 pubs deserves their place, plus they all come recommended by people who know a thing or two about good beer.

£15.99   ISBN 978-1-85249-335-6

Britain's Best Real Heritage Pubs 2nd Edition

Geoff Brandwood

This definitive listing is the result of 25 years' research by CAMRA to discover pubs that are either unaltered in 70 years or have features of truly national historic importance. Fully revised from the 2013 edition, the book boasts updated information and a new set of evocative illustrations. Among the 260 pubs, there are unspoilt country locals, Victorian drinking palaces and mighty roadhouses. The book has features describing how the pub developed and what's distinctive about pubs in different parts of the country.

£9.99   ISBN: 978-1-85249-334-9

Yorkshire's Real Heritage Pubs

Editor: Dave Gamston

This unique guide will lead you to nearly 120 pubs in Yorkshire and Humber which still have interiors or internal features of real historic significance. They range from simple rural 'time-warp' pubs to ornate Victorian drinking 'palaces' and include some of the more unsung pub interiors from the inter-war and later years that we take so much for granted.

£4.99   ISBN 978-1-85249-315-8

Real Heritage Pubs of the Midlands

Editor: Paul Ainsworth

This guide will lead you to the pubs throughout the East and West Midlands that still have interiors or internal features of real historic significance. They range from rural 'time-warp' pubs, some with no bar counters, to ornate drinking 'palaces' and include some unsung interiors from the inter-war period. The first guide of its kind for the Midlands, it champions the need to celebrate, understand and protect the genuine pub heritage we have left.

£5.99   ISBN 978-1-85249-324-0

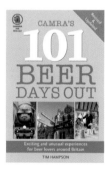

CAMRA's 101 Beer Days Out

Tim Hampson

Revised and updated for 2015, *101 Beer Days Out* is the perfect handbook for the beer tourist wanting to explore beer, pubs and brewing in the UK. From brewery tours to rail-ale trails, beer festivals to hop farms, brewing courses to historic pubs, Britain has a huge variety of beer experiences to explore and enjoy. *101 Beer Days Out* is ordered geographically, so you can easily find a beer day out wherever you are in Britain, and includes full visitor information, maps and colour photography, with detailed information on opening hours, local landmarks and public transport links to make planning any excursion quick and easy.

£12.99   ISBN 978-1-85249-328-8

London's Best Beer, Pubs & Bars – 2nd Edition
Des de Moor

The essential guide to London beer, completely revised for 2015. *London's Best Beer, Pubs & Bars* is packed with detailed maps and easy-to-use listings to help you find the best places to enjoy perfect pints in the capital. Laid out by area, the book will be your companion in exploring the best pubs serving the best British and world beers. Additional features include descriptions of London's rich history of brewing and the city's vibrant modern brewing scene, where brewery numbers have more than doubled in the last three years. The venue listings are fully illustrated with colour photographs and include a variety of real ale pubs, bars and other outlets, with detailed information to make planning any excursion quick and easy.

'*...meticulously researched and open-minded*' Will Hawkes, *The Independent*

£12.99   ISBN 978-1-85249-323-3

London Pub Walks
Bob Steel

CAMRA's pocket-size walking guide to London is back. This fully redesigned third edition is packed with updated, new pubs and new routes that take full advantage of London's public transport network. With 30 walks around more than 200 pubs, CAMRA's *London Pub Walks* enables you to explore the entire city while never being far from a decent pint.

RRP £11.99   ISBN 978-1-85249-336-3

Yorkshire Pub Walks
Bob Steel

This is a pocket-sized, traveller's guide to some of the best walking and finest pubs in Yorkshire. The walks are grouped geographically and explore some of the region's fascinating historical and literary heritage as well as its thriving brewing scene. The book contains essential information about local transport and accommodation.

£9.99 ISBN: 978-1-85249-329-5

CAMRA's So You Want to Be a Beer Expert?
Jeff Evans

More people than ever are searching for an understanding of what makes a great beer, and this book meets that demand by presenting a hands-on course in beer appreciation, with sections on understanding the beer styles of the world, beer flavours, how beer is made, the ingredients, and more. Uniquely, *So You Want to Be a Beer Expert?* doesn't just relate the facts, but helps readers reach conclusions for themselves. Key to this are the interactive tastings that show readers, through their own taste buds, what beer is all about. CAMRA's *So You Want to Be a Beer Expert?* is the ideal book for anyone who wants to further their knowledge and enjoyment of beer.

£12.99 ISBN 978-1-85249-322-6

CAMRA'S Beer Anthology

Edited by Roger Protz

An anthology of excerpts from literature, television, film and music about beer, pubs and drinking. Roger Protz, in themed chapters and using easily digested quotations, demonstrates how deeply beer and pubs are woven into the DNA of British culture. The book runs the gamut of culture, from Eastenders to Dickens, and is ideal for the casual reader looking for beer-based entertainment or for the more studious one who wants to gather a sense of how Britain's national drink – and the consumption of it – have been represented in many media.

£9.99   ISBN: 978-1-85249-333-2

CAMRA'S Beer Knowledge

Jeff Evans

With this absorbing, pocket-sized book, packed with beer facts, feats, records, stats and anecdotes, you'll never be lost for words at the pub again. More than 200 entries cover the serious, the silly and the downright bizarre from the world of beer. Inside this pint-sized compendium you'll find everything from the biggest brewer in the world to the beers with the daftest names. A quick skim before a night out and you'll always have enough beery wisdom to impress your friends.

£9.99   ISBN: 978-1-85249-338-7

CAMRA Books are available to purchase direct from the CAMRA Shop or ask at your local bookshop. Visit **www.camra.org.uk/camrabooks** or call **01727 867 201**.

Join the Campaign

CAMRA, the Campaign for Real Ale, is an independent not-for-profit, volunteer-led consumer group. We promote good-quality real ale and pubs, as well as lobbying government to champion drinkers' rights and protect local pubs as centres of community life.

CAMRA has over 185,000 members from all ages and backgrounds, brought together by a common belief in the issues that CAMRA deals with and their love of good-quality British beer. From just £25 a year – that's less than a pint a month – you can join CAMRA and enjoy the following benefits:

- A monthly colour newspaper (*What's Brewing*) and award-winning quarterly magazine (*BEER*) containing news and features about beer, pubs and brewing.

- Free or reduced entry to over 200 national, regional and local beer festivals.

- Money off many of our publications including the *Good Beer Guide* and the *Good Bottled Beer Guide*.

- A 10% discount on all holidays booked with Cottages.com and Hoseasons, a 10% discount with Beer Hawk, plus much more.

- £20 worth of J D Wetherspoon real ale vouchers* (40 x 50 pence off a pint).

- Discounts in thousands of pubs across the UK through the CAMRA Real Ale Discount Scheme.

- 15 months membership for the price of 12 for new members paying by Direct Debit**

For more details about member benefits please visit www.camra.org.uk/benefits

If you feel passionately about your pint and about pubs, join us by visiting
www.camra.org.uk/join or calling **01727 798 440**
For the latest campaigning news and to get involved in CAMRA's campaigns visit
www.camra.org.uk/campaigns

**CAMPAIGN
FOR
REAL ALE**

*Joint members receive £20 worth of J D Wetherspoon vouchers to share. **15 months membership for the price of 12 is only available the first time a member pays by Direct Debit. NOTE: Membership prices and benefits are subject to change.